Java Programming fo

By Krishna Rungt

MW00955279

Table Of Content

Chapter 1: Introduction

What is Java Platform ?

To understand JAVA programming language, we need to understand some basic concept of how a computer program can run a command and execute the action.

"Java is a programming language as well as a Platform"

How about recollecting some basic concept of computing?

What is PC?

A computer is an electronic device capable of performing computations, and we all know that it composed of a monitor, keyboard, mouse and memory to store information. But the most important component of the computer is a PROCESSOR. Which does all thinking of computer, but the question is how the computer does this thinking? How does it understand text, images, videos, etc.?

The computer is an electronic device, and it can only understand electronic signals or binary signals. For example, the 5-volt electronic signal may represent binary number 1 while 0 volts may represent binary number 0. So your PC is continuously bombarded with these signals.

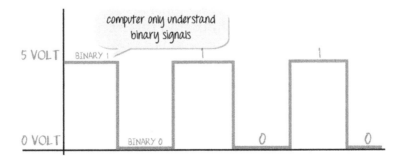

Eight bits of such signals are group together to interpret Text, numerical and symbols.

For example, the # symbol is identified by computer by 10101010. Similarly, the pattern for adding a function is represented by 10000011.

This is known as 8-bit computing. Current day processor is capable of decoding 64 bit time. But what is the relation of this concept with the programming language JAVA. Let understand these with an example.

Suppose if you want to tell the computer to add two number (1+2) which is represented by some binary numbers (10000011), how are you going to tell the computer? Yes, we going to use assembly language to get our code executed.

"Assembly Language is the most elementary form of software development languages."

We are going to give the command to a computer in this format as shown below. Your code to add two numbers in this language would be in this order.

ASSEMBLY LANGUAGE

- ☑ STORE 1 AT MEMORY LOCATION SAY A
- ☑ STORE 2 AT MEMORY LOCATION SAY B
- ☑ ADD CONTENTS OF LOCATION A & B
- ☑ STORE RESULT

- Store number 1 at memory location say A

- Store number 2 at memory location say B

- Add contents of Location A & B

- Store results

But how are we going to do this? Back in 1950's when computers were huge and consumed great deal of power, you would convert your assembly code into corresponding machine code to 1 and 0's using mapping sheets. Later these code will be punched into the machine cards and feed to the computer. The computer will read these code and execute the program. These would be a long process then until ASSEMBLER came to help.

What are Assembler and Compiler?

With the advancement in technology i/o devices were invented you could directly type your program into the PC using a program called ASSEMBLER. It converts it into corresponding machine code (110001..) and feed to your processor. So coming back to our example addition of (1+2), the assembler will convert this code into machine code and give the output.

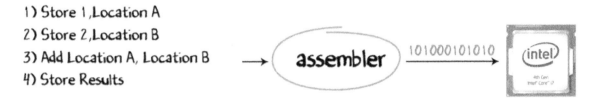

That apart, you will also have to make calls to create Operating System provided functions to display the output of the code.

But alone assembler is not involved in this whole process, it also requires the compiler to compile the long code into a small chunk of codes. With advancement in software development languages, this entire assembly code could shrink into just one line **print f 1+2 A** with the help of software called COMPILER. It is used to convert your c language code into assembly code, and the assembler converts it into corresponding machine code, and this machine code will be transmitted to the processor. The most common processor used in PC or Computers are Intel processor.

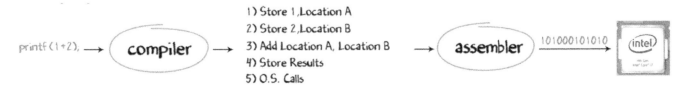

Though present day compilers come bundled with assembler can directly convert your higher language code into machine code.

Now, suppose Windows operating system is running on this Intel processor, a combination of Operating System plus the processor is called the PLATFORM. The most common platform in the world is the Windows and Intel called the Wintel Platform. The other popular platforms are AMD and **Linux** , Power PC, and Mac OS X.

Now, with a change in processor, the assembly instructions will also change. For example the

- Add instruction in Intel may be called ADDITION for AMD

- OR Math ADD for Power PC

And obviously with a change in Operating System, the level and nature of O.S level calls will also change.

As a developer, I want my software program to work on all platforms available, to maximize my revenues. So I would have to buy separate compilers which convert my print f command into the native machine code.

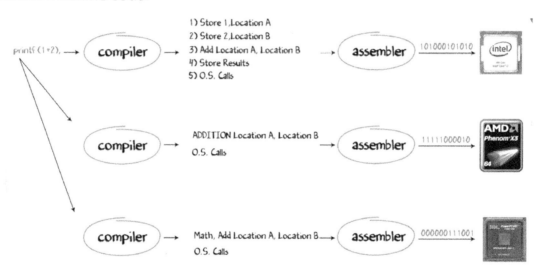

But compilers come expensive, and there is a chance of compatibility issues. So buying and installing a separate compiler for different O.S and processor is not feasible. So, what can be an alternative solution? Enter Java language.

By using **Java Virtual Machine**, these problem can be solved. But how it works on different processors and O.S. Let's understand this process step by step.

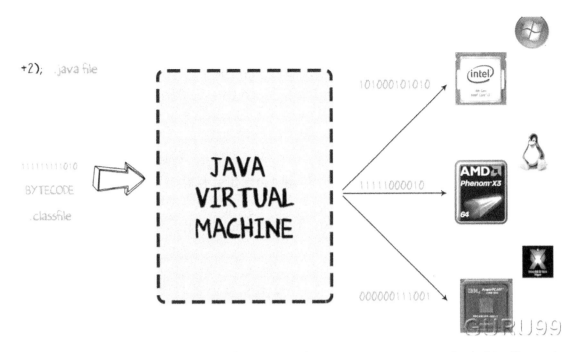

Step 1) The code to display addition of two numbers is System.out.println(1+2), and saved as .java file

Step 2) Using the java compiler the code is converted into an intermediate code called the **bytecode.** The output is a **.class file.**

Step 3) This code is not understood by any platform, but only a virtual platform called the **Java Virtual Machine**

Step 4) This Virtual Machine resides in the RAM of your operating system. When the Virtual Machine is fed with this bytecode, it identifies the platform it is working on and converts the bytecode into the native machine code

In fact, while working on your PC or browsing the web whenever you see either of these icons be assured the java virtual machine is loaded in your RAM. But what makes java lucrative is that code once compiled can run not only on all PC platforms but also mobiles or other electronic gadgets supporting java

Hence, java is a language as well as a platform (JVM)

Working of Java Virtual Machine(JVM) & its Architecture

In order to write and execute a software program you need the following
1) **Editor** – To type your program into, a notepad could be used for this
2) **Compiler** – To convert your high language program into native machine code
3) **Linker** – To combine different program files reference in your main program together.

4) Loader – To load the files from your secondary storage device like Hard Disk, Flash Drive , CD into RAM for execution. The loading is automatically done when your execute your code.
5) Execution – Actual execution of the code which is handled by your OS & processor.
With this background, refer the following video & learn the working and architecture of the Java Virtual Machine.

C code Compilation and Execution process

To understand the Java compiling process in Java. Let's first take a quick look to compiling and linking process in C.
Suppose in the main, you have called two function f1 and f2. The main function is stored in file a1.c.

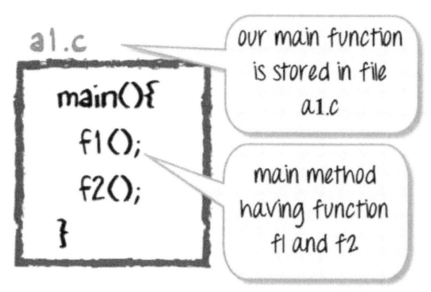

Function f1 is stored in a file a2.c

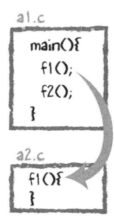

Function f2 is stored in a file a3.c

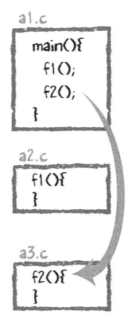

All these files, i.e., a1.c, a2.c, and a3.c, is fed to the compiler. Whose output is the corresponding object files which is the machine code.

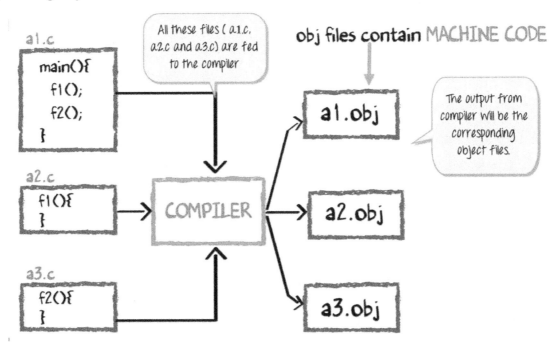

The next step is integrating all these object files into a single .exe file with the help of linker. The linker will club all these files together and produces the .exe file.

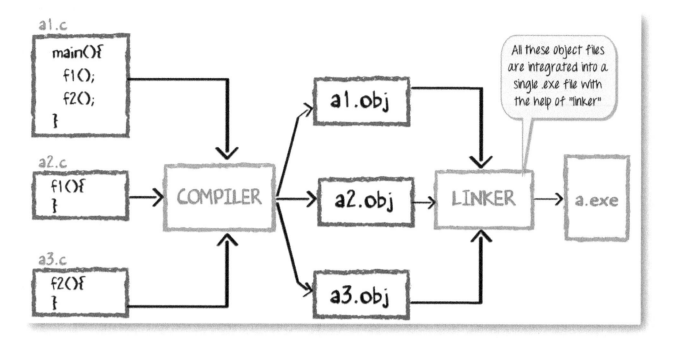

During program run a loader program will load a.exe into the RAM for the execution.

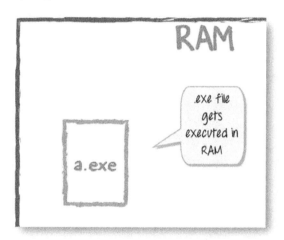

Java code compilation and execution in Java VM

Let's look at the process for JAVA. In your main you have two methods f1 and f2.

- main method is stored in file a1.java

- f1 is stored in file as a2.java

- f2 is stored in file as a3.java

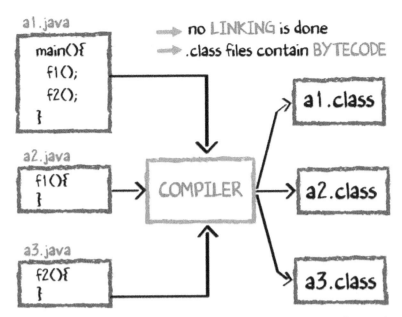

The compiler will compile the three files and produces a corresponding .class file which consists of BYTE code. **Unlike C, no linking is done**.

The Java VM or Java Virtual Machine resides on the RAM. During execution, using the class loader the class files are brought on the RAM. The BYTE code is verified for any security breaches.

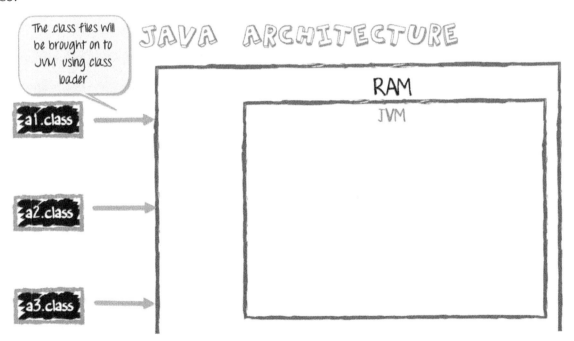

Next, the execution engine will convert the Bytecode into Native machine code. This is just in time compiling. It is one of the main reason why Java is comparatively slow.

JIT converts BYTECODE into machine code

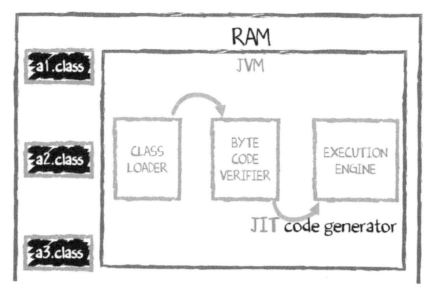

There is more to the JVM architecture which will be discussed in the later tutorial.

NOTE: JIT or Just-in-time compiler is the part of the Java Virtual Machine (JVM). It is used to speed up the execution time. It interprets part of the Byte Code that has similar functionality at the same time.

What is JVM?

JVM stands for Java Virtual Machine. It is the engine that drives the Java Code. It converts Java bytecode into machines language.

In other programming language, the compiler produces code for a particular system. But Java compiler produces code for a Virtual Machine.

In JVM, Java code is compiled into bytecode. This bytecode gets interpreted on different machines

Between host system and Java source, Bytecode is an intermediary language.

JVM is responsible for allocating a memory space.

Why is Java both interpreted and compiled language?

Programming languages are classifies as

Higher Level Language Ex. C++ , Java

Middle Level Languages Ex. C

Low Level Language Ex Assembly

finally the lowest level as the Machine Language.

A **compiler** is a program which converts a program from one level of language to another. Example conversion of C++ program into machine code.

The java compiler is a convert's high level java code into bytecode (which is also a type of machine code).

A **interpreter** is a program which converts a program at one level to another programming language at the same level. Example conversion of Java program into C++

In Java , the Just In Time Code generator converts the bytecode into the native machine code which are at the same programming levels.

Hence java is both compiled as well as interpreted language.

Why is Java slow?

The two main reasons behind the slowness of Java are

Dynamic Linking = Unlike C, linking is done at run-time , every time the program is run in Java.

Run-time Interpreter = The conversion of byte code into native machine code is done at run-time in Java which furthers slows down the speed

However, the latest version of Java have addressed the performance bottlenecks to a great extent.

Summary:

JVM or Java Virtual Machine is the engine that drives the Java Code. It converts Java bytecode into machines language.

In JVM, Java code is compiled to bytecode. This bytecode gets interpreted on different machines

JIT or Just-in-time compiler is the part of the Java Virtual Machine (JVM). It is used to speed up the execution time

In comparison to other compiler machine, Java may be slow in execution.

How to install Java JDK 8 and Java 8 download

Following are steps to install Java in Windows

Step 1) Go to **link**. Click on Download JDK. For java latest version

Java SE Downloads

Java Platform (JDK) 8u31

NetBeans with JDK 8

Java Platform, Standard Edition

Java SE 8u31
This release includes important security fixes. Oracle strongly recommends that all Java SE 8 users upgrade to this release.
Learn more ▸

- Installation Instructions
- Release Notes
- Oracle License
- Java SE Products
- Third Party Licenses
- Certified System Configurations
- Readme Files
  - JDK ReadMe
  - JRE ReadMe

JDK
DOWNLOAD ⬇

Server JRE
DOWNLOAD ⬇

JRE
DOWNLOAD ⬇

Step 2) Next,

1. Accept License Agreement

2. Download latest java JDK for your version(32 or 64 bit) of java for Windows

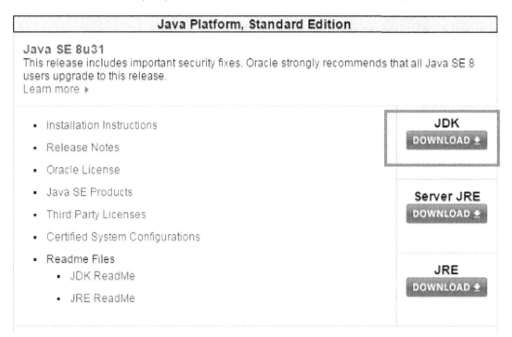

Step 3) Once the download is complete, run the exe for install jdk . Click Next

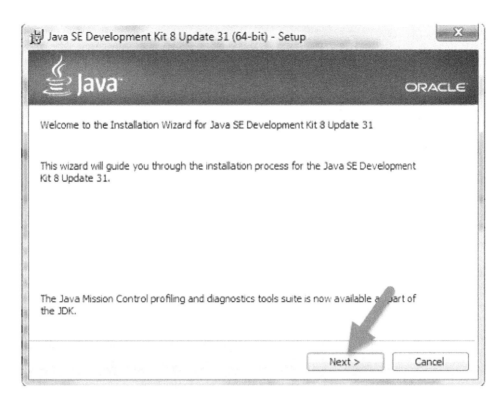

Step 4) Once install is complete click Close

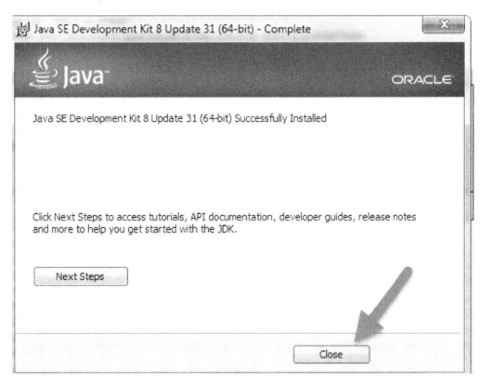

Step 5) Set Environment Variable, " PATH = <JDK installation directory>\bin;%PATH%"

For Java 1.8

PATH = C:\Program Files\Java\jdk1.8.0_31\bin;%PATH%

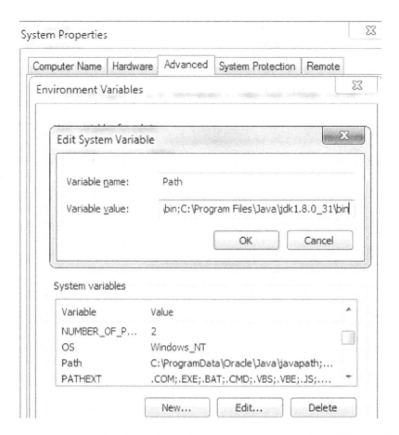

If the latest version on Java website is 1.8.0_65, your class path will be **C:\Program Files\Java\jdk1.8.0_65\bin;%PATH%**

Step 6) Set Environment Variable, "CLASSPATH = <JDK installation directory>\lib\tools.jar;"

For Java 1.8

CLASSPATH = C:\Program Files\Java\jdk1.8.0_31\lib\tools.jar;

Step 7) Restart your PC. Go to command prompt and type javac

If you see a screen like below' Java is installed.

Having trouble installing Java? Check our **Online Java Compiler**

Creating Your First Java Program

Assignment

Step 1) Copy the following code into a notepad.
```
class A {
public static void main(String args[]){
   System.out.println("First Java Program");
}
}
```
Step 2) Save the file in the directory directory **C:\workspace** , as **FirstProgram.java** in the & not as **FirstProgram.java.txt**

Step 3) Open the command prompt. Go to Directory **C:\workspace** . Compile the code using command, **javac FirstProgram.java**

Step 4) Run the code using command, **java A**

Chapter 2: OOPS

Easily understand concept of Object Oriented Programming(OOP)

Points to Remember:

- **Unstructured Programming Languages:** The most primitive of all programming languages having sequentially flow of control. Code is repeated through out the program

- **Structured Programming Languages:** Has non-sequentially flow of control. Use of functions allows for re-use of code.

- **Object Oriented Programming**: Combines Data & Action Together.

What is Abstraction in OOP?

Suppose you want to create a banking application and you are asked to collect all the information about your customer? There are chances that you will come up with many information related to a customer, but many of them are not required at least for a banking application.

So, you need to sort out the relevant information for your banking application from that pool of database like name, address, tax information, etc. Since we have fetched or sorted out the customer information from the largest Pool- hence the process is referred as Abstraction.

But the same information once extracted can be used for a wide range of applications. For instance, you can use the same data for hospital application, job portal application, Government database, etc.

Points to Remember about Java Abstraction:

- Abstraction is the process of selecting important data sets for an Object in your software , and leaving out the insignificant ones.

- Once you have modeled your object using Abstraction , the same set of data could be used in different applications.

Learn Java Encapsulation in 10 Minutes

Encapsulation is one of the four OOP concepts. The other three are Inheritance, Polymorphism, and Abstraction.

In Java, encapsulation is a mechanism of wrapping data (variables) and code together as a single unit.

To understand what is encapsulation? We will see an example of a banking application created in our previous tutorial.

Suppose a hacker managed to gain access to the code of your bank account. Now, he tries to deposit amount -100 into your account by two ways. Let see his first method or approach.

Approach 1: He tries to deposit an invalid amount (say -100) into your bank account by manipulating the code.

```
class Hacker{
Account a= new Account ();
a.account_balance= -100;
```

Now, the question is – Is that possible?

Let see whether it is possible or not? Usually, a variable and class is set as a "Private" as shown below. It can only be accessed with the corresponding methods, and no other alternatives methods are allowed to carry out the operations.

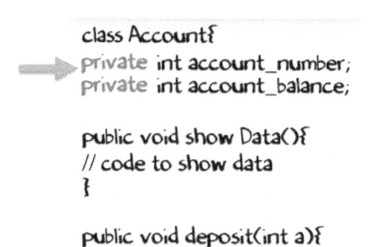

```
class Account{
  private int account_number;
  private int account_balance;

  public void show Data(){
  // code to show data
  }

  public void deposit(int a){
```

If a data member is private, it means it can only be accessed within the same class. No outside class can access private data member or variable of other class.

So in our case hacker cannot deposit amount -100 to your account.

```
class Hacker{
  Account a= new Account ();

  a.account_balance= -100;


  }
```

Approach 2: Hacker's first approach failed to deposit the amount. Next, he tries to do same by using "deposit" method. To carry out this operation he uses "deposit" method.

```
class Hacker{
  Account a= new Account

  a.account_balance= -10C

  a.deposit(-100);
  }
```

But method implementation has check for negative values. So the second approach also fails in depositing amount -100 into your account.

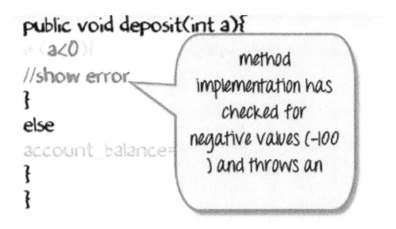

Thus, you never expose your data to an external party. Which makes your application secure.

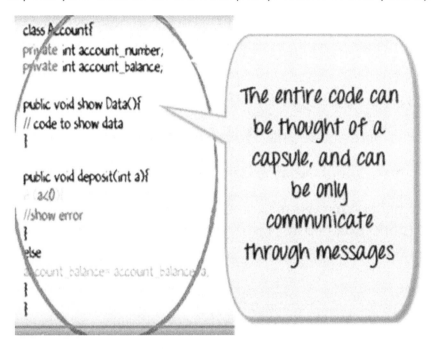

The entire code can be thought of a capsule, and you can only communicate through the messages. Hence the name encapsulation.

Few notes on Encapsulation in Java :

- In Java, encapsulation is binding the data with its related functionalities

- Here functionalities mean "methods" and data means "variables"

- So we keep variable and methods in one place. That place is "class."

- "Class" is the base for encapsulation.

- With Java Encapsulation, you can hide (restrict access) to critical data members in your code, which improves security

- As we discussed earlier, if a data member is declared "private", then it can only be accessed within the same class. No outside class can access data member (variable) of other class.

- However if you need to access these variables, you have to use **public "getter" and "setter"** methods.

- Setup public "getter" and "setter" method to update and read the private data field. This will allow data access from private class.

Frequently, java encapsulation is referred for **data hiding**. But more than data hiding, encapsulation concept is meant for better management or grouping of related data.

To achieve a lesser degree of encapsulation in Java you can use modifiers like "protected" or "public". With encapsulation, developers can change one part of the code easily without affecting other.

Often encapsulation is misunderstood with Abstraction. To get clear on this,

- Encapsulation is more about "How" to achieve that functionality

- Abstraction is more about "what" a class can do.

A simple example to understand this difference is a mobile phone. Where the complex logic in the circuit board is encapsulated in a touch screen, and the interface is provided to abstract it out.

Java Inheritance & Polymorphism

In the previous tutorial, we learned one of the three OOP concepts. i.e Java – Encapsulation.

In this tutorial, we will learn the remaining two OOP concept Inheritance in java and Polymorphism in java.

Before we go deep into what they are, first get an overview of it.

- **What is Inheritance?** - When a "class" acquires the property of another class it is known as Inheritance. For example, a child inherits the traits of parents.

- **What is Polymorphism?**- While Polymorphism means one name but many forms. For example, you have a smartphone for communication. The communication mode you choose could be anything. It can be a call, a text msg, a picture msg, mail, etc. So the goal is common that is communication, but their approach is different. This is called **Polymorphism.**

Consider the same banking application from the previous banking example.

Please be patient. The Video will load in some time. If you still face issue viewing video click **here**

We are supposed to open two different account types, one for saving and another for checking (also known as current).

Let's compare and study how we can approach coding from a **structured and object oriented programing perspective.**

- **Structural approach**: In structured programing, we will create two functions –

1. One to withdraw

2. And the other for deposit action.

Since the working of these functions remains same across the accounts.

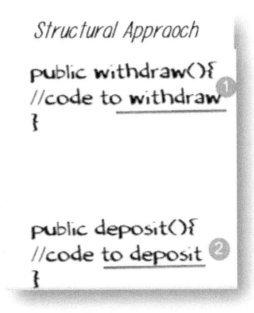

- **OOP's approach**: While using the OOPs programming approach. We would create two classes.

    o   Each having implementation of the deposit and withdraw functions.

    o   This will redundant extra work.

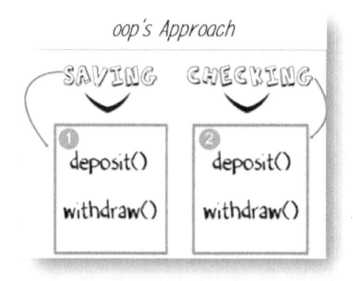

Implementing Privileged Bank Account

Now there is a change in the requirement specification for something that is so common in the software industry. You are supposed to add functionality privileged Banking Account with Overdraft Facility. For a background, overdraft is that you can withdraw an amount more than available the balance in your account.

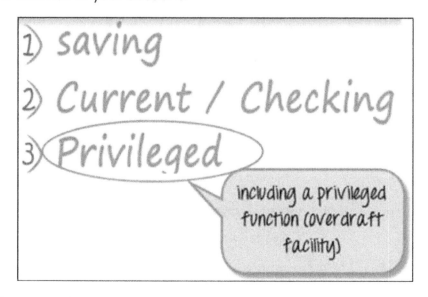

- **Structural approach:**

Using functional approach, I have to modify my withdraw function, which is already tested and baselined. And add a method like below will take care of new requirements.

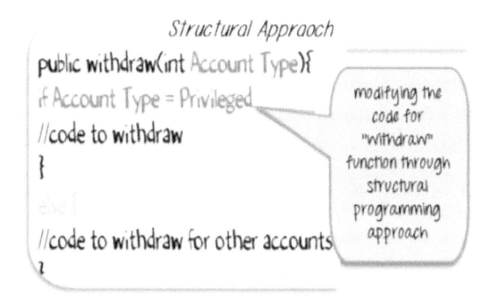

- **OOP's approach**:

  Using OOP's approach, you just need to write a new class with unique implementation of withdraw function. We never touched the tested piece of code.

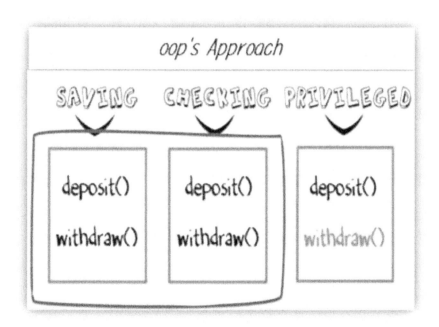

What if the requirement changes further? Like to add credit card account with its own unique requirement of deposits.

1) saving

2) Current / Checking

3) Privileged

4) Credit Card

- **Structural approach:** Using structural approach you have to change tested piece of deposit code again.

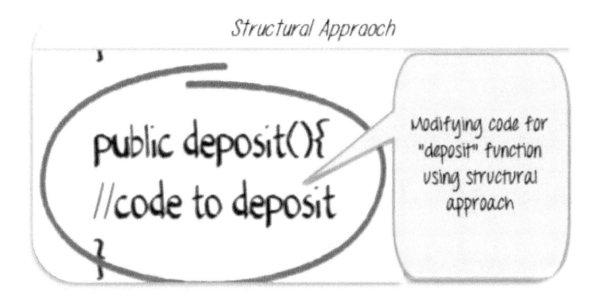

Structural Approach

```
public deposit(){
//code to deposit
}
```

Modifying code for "deposit" function using structural approach

- **OOP's approach**: But using object-oriented approach, you will just create a new class with its unique implementation of deposit method (highlighted red in the image below).

So even though the structural programming seems like an easy approach initially, OOP's wins in a long term.

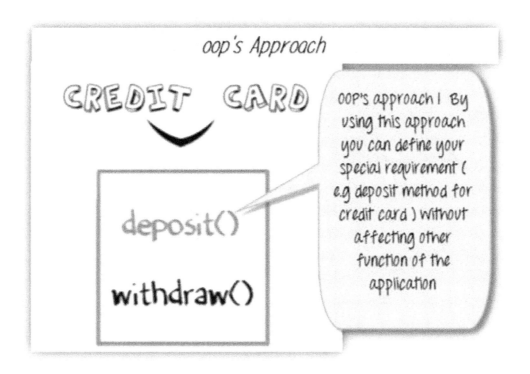

Challenge in OOP's

But one may argue that across all classes, you have a repeated pieces of code.

To overcome this, you create a parent class, say "account" and implement the same function of deposit and withdraw. And make child classes inherited "account" class. So that they will have access to withdraw and deposit functions in account class.

The functions are not required to be implemented individually. This is **Inheritance in java** .

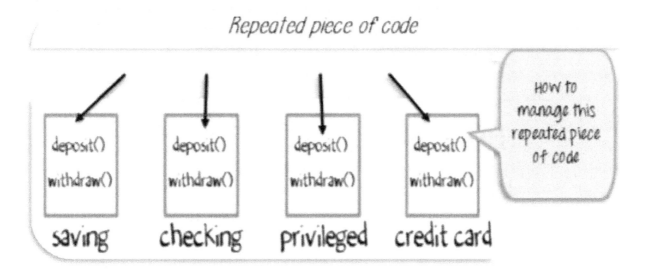

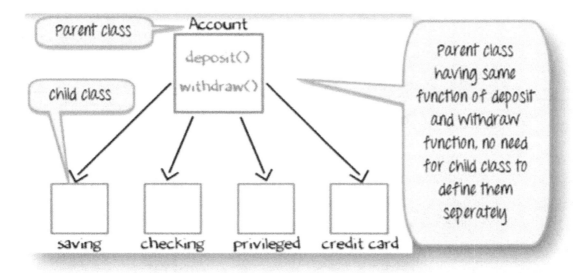

Java Polymorphism

But wait there is a problem!

Withdraw method for privileged and deposit for a credit card is different.

To overcome this, you can override the method implementation in your base(child) class.

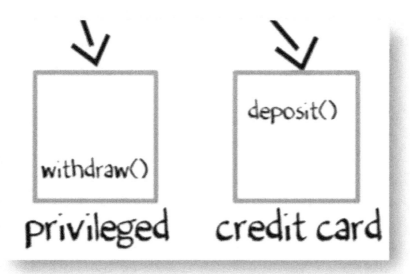

- Such that when the "withdrawn" method for saving account is called method from parent account class is executed.

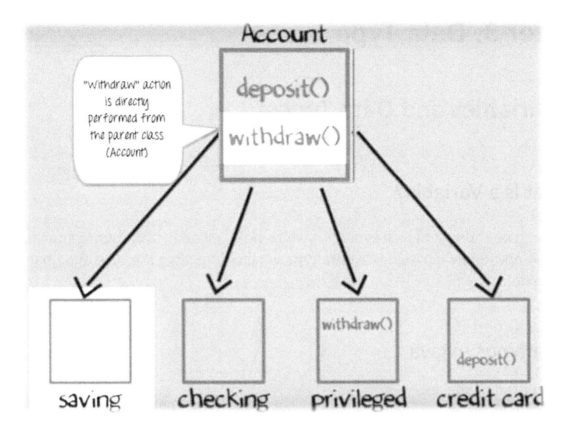

- But when the "Withdraw" method for the privileged account (overdraft facility) is called withdraw method defined in the priveldged class is executed. This is **Polymorphism**.

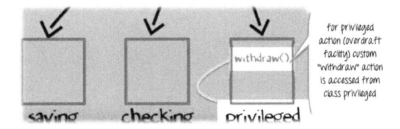

Summary:

- Encapsulation, Inheritance, and Polymorphism are all based on OOP's concept

- When a class acquires the property of another class, it is known as inheritance.

- Polymorphic means one name but many forms

- Use override method to implement the function of the derived class (child class).

Chapter 3: Data Type

Java Variables and Data Types

What is a Variable?

A variable can be thought of as a container which holds value for you during the life of your program.Every variable is assigned a **data type** which designates the type and quantity of a value it can hold.

Data types in java

The different Data Type are ---
Integer java data types
byte (1 byte)

short (2 bytes)

int (4 bytes)

long (8 bytes)

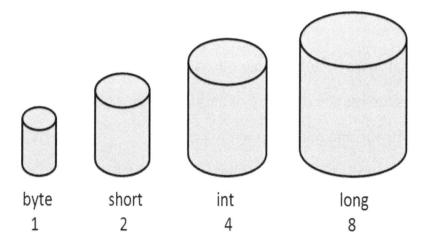

byte   short   int   long
1   2   4   8

Floating Data type

float (4 bytes)

double (8 bytes)

Textual Data Type

char (2 bytes)

Logical

boolean (1 byte) (true/false)

Points to Remember:

- All numeric data types are signed(+/-).

- The size of data types remain the same on all platforms (standardized)

- char data type in Java is 2 bytes because it uses **UNICODE** character set. By virtue of it, Java supports internationalization. UNICODE is a character set which covers all known scripts and language in the world

Variable in program need to perform 2 steps

1. Variable Declaration

2. Variable Initialization

1) Variable Declaration:

To declare a variable , you must specify the data type & give the variable a unique name.

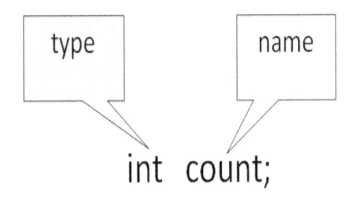

Examples of other Valid Declarations are

int a,b,c;

float pi;

double d;

char a;

2) Variable Initialization:

To initialize a variable you must assign it a valid value.

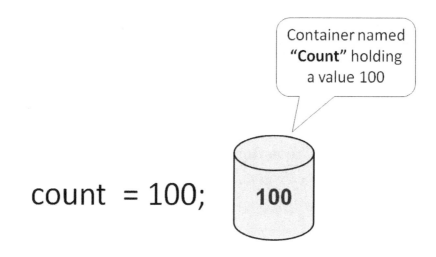

count = 100;

Example of other Valid Initializations are
pi =3.14f;

do =20.22d;

a='v';

You can combine variable declaration and initialization.

int count = 100;

Example :

int a=2,b=4,c=6;

float pi=3.14f;

double do=20.22d;

char a='v';

Java Variable Type Conversion & Type Casting

A variable of one type can receive the value of another type.Here there are 2 cases -
case 1) Variable of smaller capacity is be assigned to another variable of bigger capacity.

$$\text{double d ;}$$
$$\text{int i = 10;}$$
$$\text{d = i;}$$

This process is Automatic, and non-explicit is known as **CONVERSION**
case 2) Variable of larger capacity is be assigned to another variable of smaller capacity

$$\text{double d}\ \ = 10;$$
$$\text{int i;}$$
$$\text{i = (int) d}$$

Type Cast
Operator

In such cases you have to explicitly specify the **type cast operator. This process is known
as TYPE CASTING.**

In case, you do not specify a type cast operator, the compiler gives an error. Since this rule is enforced by the compiler , it makes the programmer aware that the conversion he is about to do may cause some loss in data and prevents **accidental losses.**

Assignment: To Understand Type Casting

Step 1) Copy the following code into an editor.

```
class Demo{
public static void main(String args[]){
byte x;
int a=270;
double b =128.128;
System.out.println("int converted to byte");
x=(byte) a;
System.out.println("a and x "+ a +" "+x);
System.out.println("double converted to int");
a=(int) b;
System.out.println("b and a "+ b +" "+a);
System.out.println("\n double converted to byte");
x= b;
System.out.println("b and x "+b +" "+x);
} }
```

Step 2) Save, Compile & Run the code.
Step 3) Error =? Try to debug. Hint - Typecasting is missing for one operation.

Objects and Classes in Java

Classes and objects are the fundamental components of OOP's. Often there is a confusion between classes and objects. In this tutorial, we try to tell you the difference between class and object.

First, let's understand what they are,

- **What is Class**: A class is an entity that determines how an object will behave and what the object will contain. In other words, it is a blueprint or a set of instruction to build a specific type of object.

- **What is an object**: An object is nothing but a self-contained component which consists of methods and properties to make a particular type of data useful. Object determines the behavior of the class. When you send a message to an object, you are asking the object to invoke or execute one of its methods.

From a programming point of view, an object can be a data structure, a variable or a function. It has a memory location allocated. The object is designed as class hierarchies.

What is the difference between Object & class?

A **class** is a **blueprint or prototype** that defines the variables and the methods (functions) common to all objects of a certain kind.

An **object** is a specimen of a class. Software objects are often used to model real-world objects you find in everyday life.

Let understand the concept of Java classes and objects with an example.

Please be patient. The Video will load in some time. If you still face issue viewing video click **here**

Let's take an example of developing a pet management system, specially meant for dogs. You will need various information about the dogs like different breeds of the dogs, the age, size, etc.

You need to model real life beings, i.e., dogs into software entities.

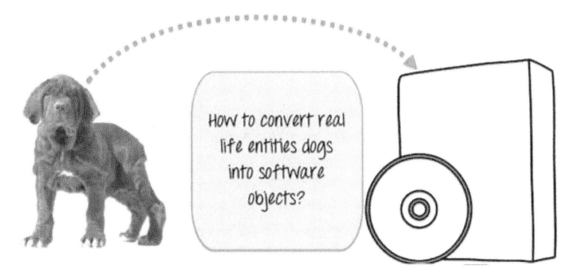

Moreover, the million dollar

question is, how you design such software?

Here is the solution-

First, let's do an exercise.

You can see the picture of three different breeds of dogs below.

Stop here right now! List down the differences between them.

Some of the differences you might have listed out may be breed, age, size, color, etc. If you think for a minute, these differences are also some common characteristics shared by these dogs. These characteristics (breed, age, size, color) can form a data members for your object.

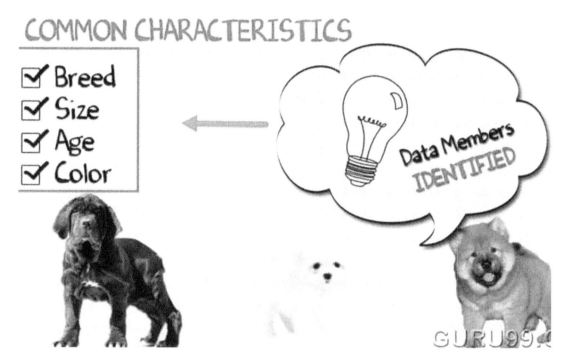

Next, list out the common behaviors of these dogs like sleep, sit, eat, etc. So these will be the actions for our software objects.

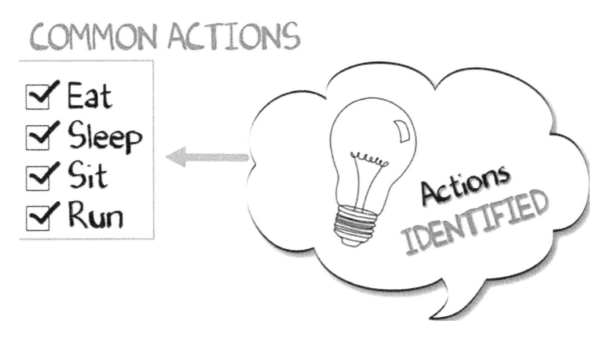

So far we have defined following things,

- Class - Dogs

- Data members or objects- size, age, color, breed, etc.

- Methods- eat, sleep, sit and run.

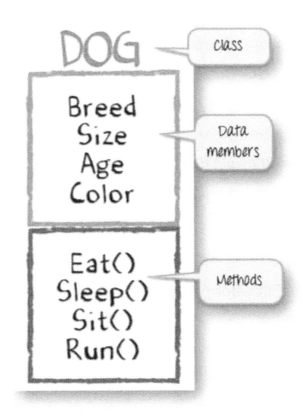

Now, for different values of data members (breed size, age, and color) in Java class, you will get different dog objects.

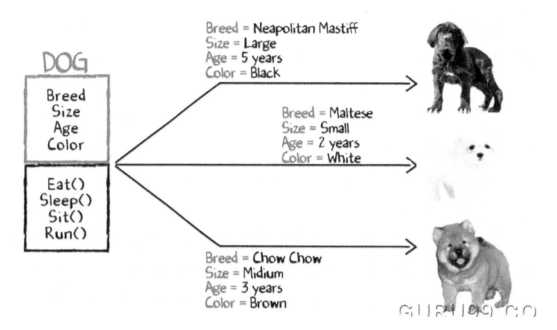

You can design any program using this OOPs approach.

While creating a class, one must follow the following principles.

- **Single Responsibility Principle (SRP)-** A class should have only one reason to change

- **Open Closed Responsibility (OCP)-** It should be able to extend any classes without modifying it

- **Liskov Substitution Responsibility (LSR)-** Derived classes must be substitutable for their base classes

- **Dependency Inversion Principle (DIP)-** Depend on abstraction and not on concretions

- **Interface Segregation Principle (ISP)-** Prepare fine grained interfaces that are client specific.

Summary:

- Java Class is an entity that determines how an object will behave and what the object will contain

- A Java object is a self-contained component which consists of methods and properties to make certain type of data useful

- A class system allows the program to define a new class (derived class) in terms of an existing class (superclass) by using a technique like inheritance, overriding and augmenting.

Java Array

What is an array?

An array is a very common type of data structure where in all elements must be of the same data type.Once defined , the size of an array is fixed and cannot increase to accommodate more elements.The first element of an array starts with zero.

In simple words it's a programming construct which helps replacing this

```
x0=0;
x1=1;
x2=2;
x3=3;
x4=4;
x5=5;
```

with this ...

```
x[0]=0;
x[1]=1;
x[2]=2;
x[3]=3;
x[4]=4;    x[5]=5;
```

how this helps is that the index (the number in the bracket[]) can be referenced by a variable for easy looping.

```
for(count=0; count<5; count++) {
    System.out.println(x[count]);
}
```

Array Variables

Using and array in your program is a **3 step process** -

1) Declaring your Array
2) Constructing your Array
3) Initializing your Array

Syntax for Declaring Array Variables

```
<elementType>[] <arrayName>;
```
or
```
;
```
Example:
```
int intArray[];
 // Defines that intArray is an ARRAY variable which will store integer values
int []intArray;
```

Constructing an Array

```
 = new [];
```
Example:
```
intArray = new int[10]; // Defines that intArray will store 10 integer values
```

Declaration and Construction combined

```
int intArray[] = new int[10];
```

Initializing an Array

```
intArray[0]=1; // Assigns an integer value 1 to the first element 0 of the array

intArray[1]=2; // Assigns an integer value 2 to the second element 1 of the array
```

Declaring and Initializing an Array

```
[]  = {};
```

Example:

```
 int intArray[] = {1, 2, 3, 4};
// Initilializes an integer array of length 4 where the first element is 1 , second element
is 2 and so on.
```

First Array Program

```
class ArrayDemo{
    public static void main(String args[]){
       int array[] = new int[7];
       for (int count=0;count<7;count++){
          array[count]=count+1;
       }
       for (int count=0;count<7;count++){
          System.out.println("array["+count+"] = "+array[count]);
       }
       //System.out.println("Length of Array  =  "+array.length);
       // array[8] =10;
       }
}
```

Step 2) Save , Compile & Run the code. Observe the Output

Step 3) If x is a reference to an array, X.LENGTH will give you the length of the array.

Uncomment line #10 . Save , Compile & Run the code.Observe the Output

Step 4) Unlike C, Java checks the boundary of an array while accessing an element in it. Java will not allow the programmer to exceed its boundary.

Uncomment line #11 . Save , Compile & Run the code.Observe the Output

Step 5) ArrayIndexOutOfBoundsException is thrown. In case of C , the same code would have shown some garbage value.

Java Arrays passed by reference

Arrays are passed to functions by reference, or as a pointer to the original. This means anything you do to the Array inside the function affects the original.
Assignment: To understand Array are passed by reference

Step 1) Copy the following code into a editor

```java
class ArrayDemo {
    public static void passByReference(String a[]){
        a[0] = "Changed";
    }

    public static void main(String args[]){
        String []b={"Apple","Mango","Orange"};
        System.out.println("Before Function Call    "+b[0]);
        ArrayDemo.passByReference(b);
        System.out.println("After Function Call    "+b[0]);
    }
}
```
Step 2) Save , Compile & Run the code. Observe the Output

Multidimensional arrays

Multidimensional arrays, are arrays of arrays.

To declare a multidimensional array variable, specify each additional index using another set of square brackets.

Ex: int twoD[ ][ ] = new int[4][5] ;

When you allocate memory for a multidimensional array, you need only specify the memory for the first (leftmost) dimension.

You can allocate the remaining dimensions separately.

In Java, array length of each array in a multidimensional array is under your control.

Ex:

```java
int twoD[][] = new int[4][];

twoD[0] = new int[5];

twoD[1] = new int[6];

twoD[2] = new int[7];

twoD[3] = new int[8];
```

Array of Objects

It is possible to declare array of reference variables.

Syntax:

```
Class  = new Class[array_length]
```

Assignment: To create Array Of Objects

Step 1) Copy the following code into a editor

```java
class ObjectArray{
    public static void main(String args[]){
      Account obj[] = new Account[2] ;
      //obj[0] = new Account();
      //obj[1] = new Account();
     obj[0].setData(1,2);
     obj[1].setData(3,4);
     System.out.println("For Array Element 0");
     obj[0].showData();
     System.out.println("For Array Element 1");
      obj[1].showData();
   }
}
class Account{
  int a;
  int b;
 public void setData(int c,int d){
   a=c;
   b=d;
 }
 public void showData(){
   System.out.println("Value of a ="+a);
   System.out.println("Value of b ="+b);
 }
}
```

Step 2) Save , Compile & Run the Code.

Step 3) Error= ? Try and debug before proceeding to step 4.

Step 4) The line of code , Account obj[] = new Account[2] ; exactly creates an array of two reference variables as shown below

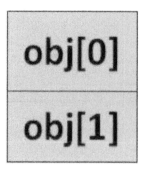

Step 5) Uncomment Line # 4 & 5. This step creates objects and assigns them to the reference variable array as shown below. Your code must run now.

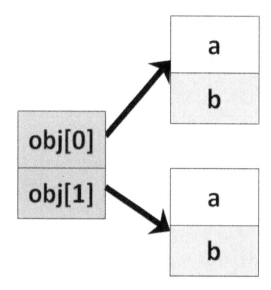

Java String Tutorial

What are Strings?

A string in literal terms is a series of characters. Hey, did you say characters, isn't it a primitive data type in Java. Yes, so in technical terms, the basic Java String is basically an array of characters.

So my above string of "**ROSE**" can be represented as the following –

Why use Strings ?

One of the primary functions of modern computer science, is processing human language

Similarly to how numbers are important to math, language symbols are important to meaning and decision making. Although it may not be visible to computer users, computers process language in the background as precisely and accurately as a calculator. Help dialogs provide instructions. Menus provide choices. And data displays show statuses, errors, and real-time changes with language.

As a Java programmer, one of your main tools for storing and processing language is going to be the String class.

String Syntax Examples

Now, let's get to some syntax, after all we need to write this in Java code isn't it.

String is an array of characters, represented as:

```
//String is an array of characters
char[] arrSample = {'R', 'O', 'S', 'E'};
String strSample_1 = new String (arrSample);
```

In technical terms, the String is defined as follows in the above example-

= new (argument);

Now we always cannot write our strings as arrays, hence we can define the String in Java as follows:

```
//Representation of String
String strSample_2 = "ROSE";
```

In technical terms, the above is represented as:

= ;

The **String Class** Java **extends** the **Object class** as shown below.

String Concatenation:

Concatenation is joining of two or more strings.

Have a look at the below picture-

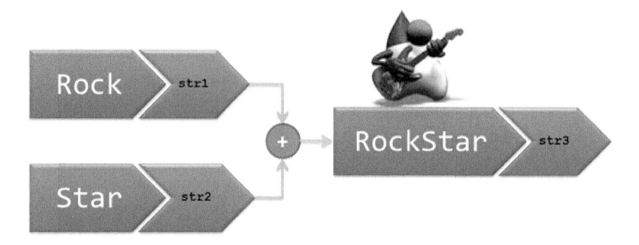

We have two strings str1 = "Rock" and str2 = "Star"

If we add up these two strings we should be having a result as str3= "RockStar".

Check the below code snippet, it explains the two methods to perform string concatenation.

First is using "**concat**" method of String class and second is using arithmetic "+" operator. Both results in the same output

```java
public class Sample_String{
  public static void main(String[] args){
//String Concatenation
String str1 = "Rock";
String str2 = "Star";
//Method 1 : Using concat
String str3 = str1.concat(str2);
System.out.println(str3);
//Method 2 : Using "+" operator
String str4 = str1 + str2;
System.out.println(str4);
}
}
```

Important Java string methods :

Hey!!   You turned me into a
Rockstar in the last topic.

There are quite some more methods
in the String class which are very
helpful too.

Let's check them out in this topic.

Let's ask the Java String class a few questions and see if it can answer them ;)

String "Length" Method

How will you determine the length of given String? I have provided a method called as "length". Use it against the String you need to find the length.

```
public class Sample_String{
  public static void main(String[] args){  //Our sample string for this tutorial
  String str_Sample = "RockStar";
  //Length of a String
  System.out.println("Length of String: " + str_Sample.length());}}
```

String "indexOf" Method

If I know the length, how would I find which character is at which position? In short, how will I find the index of a character?

You gave the answer yourself buddy, there is a "indexOf" method that will help you determine the location of a specific character that you specify.

```
public class Sample_String{
  public static void main(String[] args){//Character at position
```

```
String str_Sample = "RockStar";
System.out.println("Character at position 5: " + str_Sample.charAt(5));
//Index of a given character
System.out.println("Index of character 'S': " + str_Sample.indexOf('S'));}}
```

String "charAt" Method

Similar to the above question, given the index, how do I know the character at that location?

Simple one again!! Use the "charAt" method and provide the index whose character you need to find.

```
public class Sample_String{
  public static void main(String[] args){//Character at position
String str_Sample = "RockStar";
System.out.println("Character at position 5: " + str_Sample.charAt(5));}}
```

String "CompareTo" Method

I want to check if the String that was generated by some method is equal to something that I want to verify with? How do I compare two Strings?

Use the method "compareTo" and specify the String that you would like to compare.

Use "compareToIgnoreCase" in case you don't want the result to be case sensitive.

The result will have the value 0 if the argument string is equal to this string; a value less than 0 if this string is lexicographically less than the string argument; and a value greater than 0 if this string is lexicographically greater than the string argument.

```
public class Sample_String{
  public static void main(String[] args){//Compare to a String
String str_Sample = "RockStar";
 System.out.println("Compare To 'ROCKSTAR': " + str_Sample.compareTo("rockstar"));
 //Compare to - Ignore case
 System.out.println("Compare To 'ROCKSTAR' - Case Ignored: " + str_Sample.compareToIgnoreCase("ROCKSTAR"));}}
```

String "Contain" Method

I partially know what the string should have contained, how do I confirm if the String contains a sequence of characters I specify?

Use the method "contains" and specify the characters you need to check.

Returns **true** if and only if this string contains the specified sequence of char values.

```
public class Sample_String{
  public static void main(String[] args){  //Check if String contains a sequence
String str_Sample = "RockStar";
  System.out.println("Contains sequence 'tar': " + str_Sample.contains("tar"));}}
```

String "endsWith" Method

How do I confirm if a String ends with a particular suffix? Again you answered it. Use the "endsWith" method and specify the suffix in the arguments.

Returns **true** if the character sequence represented by the argument is a suffix of the character sequence represented by this object.

```
public class Sample_String{
  public static void main(String[] args){  //Check if ends with a particular sequence
String str_Sample = "RockStar";
  System.out.println("EndsWith character 'r': " + str_Sample.endsWith("r"));}}
```

String "replaceAll" & "replaceFirst" Method

I want to modify my String at several places and replace several parts of the String?

Java String Replace, replaceAll and replaceFirst methods. You can specify the part of the String you want to replace and the replacement String in the arguments.

```
public class Sample_String{
  public static void main(String[] args){//Replace Rock with the word Duke
String str_Sample = "RockStar";
System.out.println("Replace 'Rock' with 'Duke': " + str_Sample.replace("Rock", "Duke"));}}
```

String Java "tolowercase" & Java "touppercase"

I want my entire String to be shown in lower case or Upper case?

Just use the "toLowercase()" or "ToUpperCase()" methods against the Strings that need to be converted.

```
public class Sample_String{
  public static void main(String[] args){//Convert to LowerCase
String str_Sample = "RockStar";
System.out.println("Convert to LowerCase: " + str_Sample.toLowerCase());
//Convert to UpperCase
System.out.println("Convert to UpperCase: " + str_Sample.toUpperCase());}}
```

Important Points to Note:

- **String is a Final class**; i.e once created the value cannot be altered. Thus String objects are called immutable.

- The Java Virtual Machine(JVM) creates a memory location especially for Strings called **String Constant Pool**. That's why String can be initialized without 'new' key word.

- String class falls under **java.lang.String hierarchy**. But there is no need to import this class. Java platform provides them automatically.

- String **reference can be overridden but that does not delete the content**; i.e., if

String h1 = "hello";

h1 = "hello"+"world";

then "hello" String does not get deleted. It just looses its handle.

- **Multiple references** can be used for same String but it will **occur in the same place**; i.e., if

String h1 = "hello";

String h2 = "hello";

String h3 = "hello";

then only one pool for String "hello" is created in the memory with 3 references-h1,h2,h3

- If a **number is quoted in " "** then it **becomes a string**, not a number any more. That means if

String S1 ="The number is: "+ "123"+"456";

System.OUT.println(S1);

then it will print: The number is: 123456

If the initialization is like this:

String S1 = "The number is: "+(123+456);

System.OUT.println(S1);

then it will print: The number is:579 That's all to Strings!

How to convert a Java String to Integer?

There are many ways you can do this, but the easiest way is simply use the method Integer.parseInt().

Hey Duke – My client sends me information in XML. The XML contains numbers. But when I read the data, it's not an integer but String!

I need to perform some arithmetic operation on the XML. But I cannot do them on strings. How do I convert Strings

So you are back!

Sure, you see Java provides a method known as ParseInt that does exactly what you are looking for. Let's check this in detail.

Example:
Let's say you have a string – strTest - that contains a numeric value.

String strTest = "100";

Try to perform some arithmetic operation like divide by 4 – This immediately shows you a compilation error.

Example : Integer.parseInt()

Now make use of ParseInt method as follows:

int <IntVariableName> = Integer.parseInt(<StringVariableName>);

Pass the string variable as the argument.

This will convert the java String to java Integer and store it into the specified integer variable

Check the below code snippaet-

Java Example: String to Integer

```
class StrConvert{
  public static void main(String []args){
    String strTest = "100";
    //This statement results in a compilation error as you
    //cannot do arithmetic operation on Strings
```

```
//System.out.println("Using String:" + (strTest/4));
//Convert the String to Integer
int iTest = Integer.parseInt(strTest);
System.out.println("Actual String:"+ strTest);
System.out.println("Converted to Int:" + iTest);
//This will now show some arithmetic operation
System.out.println("Arithmetic Operation on Int:" + (iTest/4));
  }
}
```

Working with HashMap in Java

What is Hashmap in Java?

A HashMap basically designates **unique keys** to corresponding **values**that can be retrieved at any

given point.

Features of Java Hashmap

a) The **values** can be stored in a map by forming a **key-value** pair. The value can be retrieved using the key by passing it to the correct method.

b) If **no element** exists in the Map, it will throw a '**NoSuchElementException**'.

c) HashMap stores only **object references**. That's why, it's impossible to use **primitive data types** like double or int. Use wrapper class (like Integer or Double) instead.

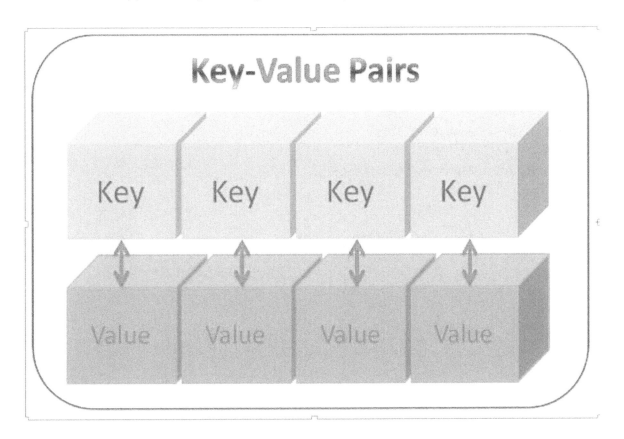

Using HashMaps in Java Programs:

Following are the two ways to declare a Hash Map:

```
HashMap<String, Object> map = new HashMap<String, Object>();
HashMap<String, Object> map = new HashMap<String, Object>();
```

Important Hashmap Methods

- **get(Object KEY)** – This will return the value associated with specified key in this Java hashmap.

- **put(Object KEY, String VALUE)** – This method stores the specified value and associates it with the specified key in this map.

Java Hashmap Example

Following is a sample implementation of java Hash Map:

```java
import java.util.HashMap;
import java.util.Map;
public class Sample_TestMaps{
  public static void main(String[] args){
    Map<String, String> objMap = new HashMap<String, String>();
    objMap.put("Name", "Suzuki");
    objMap.put("Power", "220");
    objMap.put("Type", "2-wheeler");
    objMap.put("Price", "85000");
    System.out.println("Elements of the Map:");
    System.out.println(objMap);
  }
}
```

Lets us ask a few queries to the Hash Map itself to know it better

Q: So Mr.Hash Map, how can I find if a particular key has been assigned to you?

A: Cool, you can use the containsKey(Object KEY) method with me, it will return a Boolean value if I have a value for the given key.

Q: How do I find all the available keys that are present in the Map?

A: I have a method called as **keyset**() that will return all the keys in the map. In the above example, if you write a line as – **System.out.println(objMap.keySet());**

It will return an **output** as-
[Name, Type, Power, Price]

Similarly, if you need all the values only, I have a method as **values**().
System.out.println(objMap.values());

It will return an **output** as-
[Suzuki, 2-wheeler, 220, 85000]

Q: Suppose, I need to remove only a particular key from the Map, do I need to delete the entire Map?

A: No buddy!! I have a method as **remove**(Object KEY) that will remove only that particular key-value pair.

Q: How can we check if you actually contain some key-value pairs?

A: Just check if I am empty or not!! In short, use **isEmpty**() method against me ;)

How to use Java Arraylist

What is ArrayList in Java?

Wondering how ArrayList java could be useful , see the below conversation -

Hey Duke, I am facing a small challenge in my program. I have a series of elements that I need to handle on a dynamic basis. Sometimes it can be 5 elements, sometimes 3 or at times 10 too. Can you please suggest a suitable solution wherein I can handle this dynamic behavior efficiently?

Of course!! I can help on that, you see we knew that such situations will arise several times and we have a very useful structure called as ArrayList for this purpose. Let's understand this in

See the following picture of a man stretching an elastic rubber band.

The actual length of the rubber band is much smaller but when stretched it can extend a lot more than its actual length and can be used to hold/bind much larger objects with it.

Now, consider the next picture, that of a simple rope, it cannot stretch and will have a fixed length.

Arraylist are like **RubberBands**

Arrays are like a rope.

They are fixed

It can grow as and when required to accommodate the elements it needs to store and when elements are removed, it can shrink back to a smaller size.

So as our friend has an issue like the array he is using cannot be expanded or made to shrink, we will definitely be using ArrayList.

Arrays are like the rope shown in the above picture; they will have a fixed length, cannot be expanded nor reduced from the original length.

So our stretchable rubber-band is much like the Array List whereas the rope can be considered as the array.

Technically speaking, java Array List is like a dynamic array or a variable-length array.

Let us see and understand the following code snippet that will help you working around with Array List.

ArrayList<Object> a = new ArrayList<Object>();

Arraylist Methods

- **Arraylist add**: This is used to add elements to the Array List. If an ArrayList already contains elements, the new element gets added after the last element unless the index is specified.

- **Arraylist remove**: The specified element is removed from the list and the size is reduced accordingly. Alternately, you can also specify the index of the element to be removed.

- **Java array size**: This will give you the number of elements in the Array List. Just like arrays, here too the first element starts with index 0.

- **Arraylistcontains**: This method will return true if the list contains the specified element.

Java Arraylist Example

```java
import java.util.ArrayList;
class Test_ArrayList {
    public static void main(String[] args) {
        //Creating a generic ArrayList
        ArrayList arlTest = new ArrayList();
        //Size of arrayList
        System.out.println("Size of ArrayList at creation: " +  arlTest.size());
        //Lets add some elements to it
        arlTest.add("D");
        arlTest.add("U");
        arlTest.add("K");
        arlTest.add("E");

        //Recheck the size after adding elements
        System.out.println("Size of ArrayList after adding elements: " + arlTest.size());

        //Display all contents of ArrayList
        System.out.println("List of all elements: " + arlTest);

        //Remove some elements from the list
```

```java
        arlTest.remove("D");
        System.out.println("See contents after removing one element: " + arlTest);


        //Remove element by index
        arlTest.remove(2);
        System.out.println("See contents after removing element by index: " + arlTest);


        //Check size after removing elements
        System.out.println("Size of arrayList after removing elements: " + arlTest.size());
        System.out.println("List of all elements after removing elements: " + arlTest);


        //Check if the list contains "K"
        System.out.println(arlTest.contains("K"));


    }
}
```

Note: For simplicity, the elements shown in above code are single character elements. We can add Strings, integers etc too.

Does that solve your problem buddy? Here's ArrayList for you now!!

Cool Duke!

I am really thankful to you; I will explore more

Chapter 4: Must Know Stuff!

Java "THIS" Keyword

Keyword **'THIS'** in Java is a reference variable that refers to the current object.

The various usage of keyword Java 'THIS' in Java is as per the below,

- It can be used to refer current class instance variable

- It can be used to invoke or initiate current class constructor

- It can be passed as an argument in the method call

- It can be passed as argument in the constructor call

- It can be used to return the current class instance

```java
class Account{                                        ①
int a;
int b;                ②
public void setData(int a ,int b){            ③
a = a;
b = b;

}

public void showData(){              ④
System.out.println("Value of A ="+a);
System.out.println("Value of B ="+b);
}

public static void main(String [args]){
Account obj = new Account();          ⑤
obj.setData(2,3);
obj.showData();
}

}
```

1. **Class**: Let's create a class Account with

2. **InstanceVariable**: a and b and

3. **Method Set data**: To set the value for a and b.

4. **Method Show data**: To display the values for a and b.

5. **Main method:** where we create an object for Account class and call methods set data and show data.

Let's compile and run the code

Our expected output for A and B should be initialized to the values 2 and 3 respectively.

But the value is 0, Why? let's investigate.

In the method Set data, the arguments are declared as a and b, while the instance variables are also named as a and b.

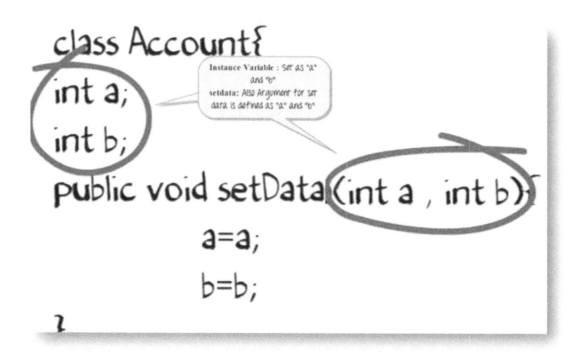

During execution, the complier is confused. Whether "a" on the left side of the assigned operator is the instance variable or the local variable. Hence, it is not set the value of 'a' when the method set data is called.

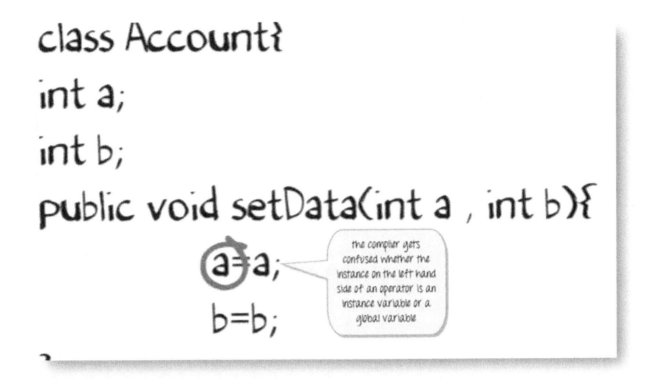

So, problem can be overcome by "THIS" keyword

Append both 'a' and 'b' with the "this" keyword followed by a dot (.) operator.

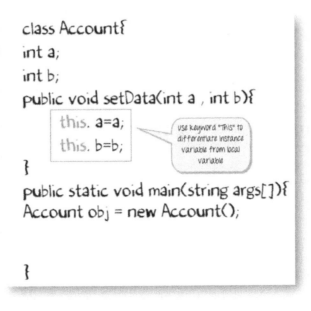

```
public void setData(int a , int b){
        this. a=a;
        this. b=b;
}
```

> after declaring "this" keyword, now we will call the setdata method, and see what happens...

```
public static void main(String args[]){
Account obj = new Account();
        obj.setData(2,3);
```

During code execution when an object calls the method 'setdata'. The keyword 'this' is replaced by the object handler "obj." (See the image below).

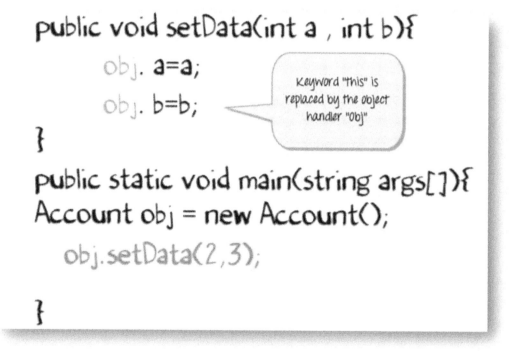

So now the compiler know,

- The 'a' on the left-hand side is an Instance variable.

- Whereas the 'a' on right-hand side is a local variable

The variables are initialized correctly, and the expected output is shown.

```
C:\workspace>javac thisDemo.java

C:\workspace>java Account
Value of A=2
Value of B=3
```

Suppose you are smart enough to choose different names for your instance variable and methods arguments.

But this time around, you create two objects of the class, each calling the set data method.

How the compiler will determine whether it is supposed to work on instance variable of object 1 or object 2.

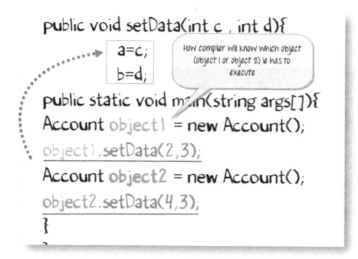

Well, the **compiler implicitly appends** the instance variable with "THIS" keyword (image below). Such that when object 1 is calling a set data method, instance variable are appended by its reference variable. While object 2 is calling the set data method, an instance variable of object 2 are modified.

```
public void setData(int c , int d){
    this.a=c;
    this.b=d;
```
use keyword "this" infront of instance variable
```
public static void main(string args[]){
Account object1 = new Account();
object1.setData(2,3);
Account object2 = new Account();
object2.setData(4,3);
}
}
```

```java
public void setData(int c , int d){
    object1.a=c;
    object1.b=d;
```

"this" keyword is replaced by the object that has to be executed. Here it is replaced by obj 1

```java
public static void main(string args[]){
Account object1 = new Account();
object1.setData(2,3);

Account object2 = new Account();
object2.setData(4,3);
}
```

```java
public void setData(int c , int d){
    object2.a=c;
    object2.b=d;
```

Likewise object 2 can replace "this" keyword

```java
public static void main(string args[]){
Account object1 = new Account();
object1.setData(2,3);

Account object2 = new Account();
object2.setData(4,3);
}
```

This process is taken care by the compiler itself. You don't have to append 'this' keyword explicitly unless there is an exceptional situation as in our example.

Points to Remember:

- "this" is a reference to the current object, whose method is being called upon.

- You can use "this" keyword to avoid naming conflicts in the method/constructor of your instance/object.

Assignment: To learn the use "this" keyword

Step 1) Copy the following code into a notepad.

```java
class Account{
int a;
int b;

 public void setData(int a ,int b){
  a = a;
  b = b;
 }
 public void showData(){
   System.out.println("Value of A ="+a);
   System.out.println("Value of B ="+b);
 }
 public static void main(String args[]){
   Account obj = new Account();
   obj.setData(2,3);
   obj.showData();
 }
}
```

Step 2) Save ,Compile & Run the code.

Step 3) Value of a & b is shown as zero ? To correct the error append line # 6 & 7with "**this**" keyword.

```java
this.a =a;
this.b=b;
```

Step 4) Save ,Compile & Run the code. This time around , values of a & b are set to 2 & 3 respectively.

Summary:

- Keyword **'THIS'** in Java is a reference variable that refers to the current object.

- It can be used to refer current class instance variable

- It can be used to invoke or initiate current class constructor

- It can be passed as an argument in the method call

- It can be passed as argument in the constructor call

- It can be used to return the current class instance

Java Command Line Arguments

What is Command Line Argument?

During program execution, information passed following a programs name in the command line is called Command Line Arguments.

Example
While running a class **Demo**, you can specify command line arguments as

java Demo arg1 arg2 arg3 ...

Command Line Arguments in Java: Important Points

- Command Line Arguments can be used to specify configuration information while launching your application.

- There is no restriction on the number of java command line arguments.You can specify any number of arguments

- Information is passed as Strings.

- They are captured into the String args of your main method

Assignment: To Learn java Command Line Arguments

Step 1) Copy the following code into a editor

```
class Demo{
    public static void main(String b[]){
        System.out.println("Argument one = "+b[0]);
        System.out.println("Argument two = "+b[1]);
    }
}
```
Step 2) Save & Compile the code

Step 3) Run the code as **java Demo apple orange**

Step 4) You must get an output as below.

Chapter 5: Java Inheritance

Java Abstract Class and Methods

Concept of Abstract Class

Consider the following class hierarchy consisting of a Shape class which is inherited by three classes Rectangle , Circle and Triangle. The Shape class is created to save on common attributes and methods shared by the three classes Rectangle , Circle and Triangle. calculateArea() is one such method shared by all 3 child classes and present in Shape class.

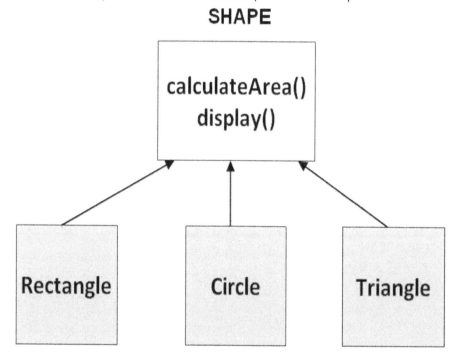

Now, assume you write code to create objects for the classes depicted above. Lets observe how these **objects will look in a practical world.**

An object of the class rectangle, will gives a rectangle , a shape we so commonly observed in everyday life

Rectangle obj = new Rectangle();

An object of the class triangle, will gives a triangle , again a common everyday shape

Triangle obj = new Triangle();

But what would an object of Class Shape look like in a practical world ??

Shape obj = new Shape();

???

If you observe the Shape class serves in **our goal of achieving inheritance and polymorphism** . But it was not built to be instantiated.Such classes can be labeled **Abstract**.An abstract class can not be instantiated.

Ex.

```
abstract class Shape{
// code
}
```

It is possible that you DO NOT label Shape class as Abstract and then instantiate it. But such object will have no use in your code and will open a room for potential errors. Hence this is not desirable.

Abstract Method Java

As we all know, the formula for calculation area for rectangle , circle & triangle is different. The calculateArea() method will have to be overridden by the inheriting classes.It makes so sense defining it in the Shape class, **but we need to make sure that all the inheriting classes do have the method.**

Such methods can be labeled **abstract**.

```
abstract public void calculateArea();
```

For an **abstract method , no implementation for is required**. Only the signature of the method is defined.

Abstract Class in Java: Important Points

- An abstract class **may** also have concrete (complete) methods.

- For design purpose, a class can be declared abstract even if it does not contain any abstract methods

- Reference of an abstract class can point to objects of its sub-classes thereby achieving run-time polymorphism Ex: Shape obj = new Rectangle();

- A class must be compulsorily labeled abstract , if it has one or more abstract methods.

Final in Java

The final modifier applies to classes, methods, and variables. The meaning of final varies from context to context, but the essential idea is the same.

- A final class may not be inherited

- A final variable becomes a constant and its value can not be changed.

- A final method may not be overridden. This is done for security reasons and these methods are used for optimization.

- A final class can not be inherited

Assignment:-To learn abstract & final keywords

Step 1) Copy the following code into an Editor

```
abstract class Shape{
  final int b = 20;
  public void display(){
    System.out.println("This is display method");
  }
  abstract public void calculateArea();
}

class Rectangle extends Shape{
  public static void main(String args[]){
    Rectangle obj = new Rectangle();
    obj.display();
    //obj.b=200;
  }
}
```

Step 2) Save , Compile & Run the code.

Step 3) Error = ? The abstract method is not implemented int the class Rectangle . Fix the issue and execute the code again.

Step 4) Uncomment line # 13 . Save & Compile the code.

Step 5) Error = ? variable b is final

Concept of Inheritance Java and Java Polymorphism

Before you begin with this lesson , we recommend you you go through our earlier tutorial for **Inheritance & Polymorphism**

Inheritance in java

- When a "Is-A" relationship exists between two classes we use Inheritance

- The parent class is termed super class and the inherited class is the sub class>

- The keyword extend java is used by the sub class to inherit the features of super class

- Inheritance is important since it leads to reusability of code

Inheritance Java Example

```
class Doctor
// Instance Variables and Methods for the Doctor Class
}

class Surgeon extends Doctor{
// Inherits instance variables & methods of the doctor class
//may have variables and methods of its own.
}
```

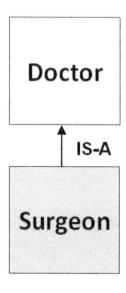

Method Overriding

Redefining a super class method in a sub class is called method overriding

Rules for Method Overriding

- The method signature i.e. method name, parameter list and return type have to match exactly.

- The overridden method can widen the accessibility but not narrow it, i.e. if it is private in the base class, the child class can make it public but not vice versa.

Example

```
Doctor doctorObj = new Doctor()
doctorObj.treatPatient()
// treatPatient method
// in class Doctor will be executed
Surgeon surgeonObj = new Surgeon();
surgeonObj.treatPatient()
// treatPatient  method
// in class Surgeon  will be executed
```

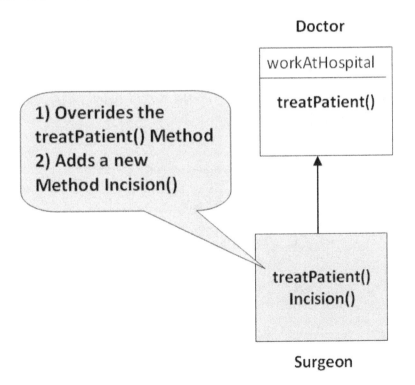

Dynamic Polymorphism Java

A reference variable of the super class can refer to a sub class object

```
Doctor obj = new Surgeon();
```

Consider the statement

```
obj.treatPatient();
```

Here the reference variable "obj" is of the parent class , but the object it is poiting to is of the child class (as show in diagram).

obj.treatPatient() will execute treatPatient() method of the sub-class - Surgeon

If a base class reference is used to call a method, the method to be invoked is decided by the JVM, depending on the object the reference is pointing to

For example, even though obj is a reference to Doctor, it calls the method of Surgeon, as it points to a Surgeon object

This is decided during run-time and hence termed **DYNAMIC** or **RUN-TIME POLYMORPHISM**

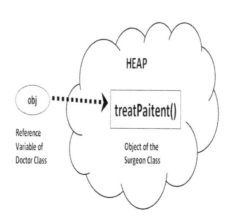

Super

What if the treatPatient method in the Surgeon class wants to do the functionality defined in Doctor class and then perform its own specific functionality?

In this case keyword **super** can be used to access methods of the parent class from the child class.

The treatPatient method in the Surgeon class could be written as:

```
treatPatient(){
  super.treatPatient();
    //add code specific to Surgeon
}
```

The keyword super can be used to access any data member or methods of the super class in the sub class.

Assignment:-To learn Inheritance , Polymorphism & super keyword

Step 1) Copy the following code into an Editor

```
public class Test{
    public static void main(String args[]){
      X x= new X();
      Y y = new  Y();
      y.m2();
     //x.m1();
      //y.m1();
     //x = y;// parent pointing to object of child
      //x.m1() ;
      //y.a=10;
     }

}
class X{
  private int a;
  int b;
    public void m1(){
      System.out.println("This is method m1 of class X");
    }
}

class Y extends X{
```

```
    int c; // new instance variable of class Y
      public void m1(){
        // overriden method
        System.out.println("This is method m1 of class Y");
      }
      public void m2(){
        super.m1();
        System.out.println("This is method m2 of class Y");
      }
}
```

Step 2) Save , Compile & Run the code. Observe the output.

Step 3) Uncomments lines # 6-9. Save , Compile & Run the code. Observe the output.

Step 4) Uncomment line # 10 . Save & Compile the code.

Step 5) Error = ? This is because sub-class can not access private members of the super class.

Difference between Overloading and overriding

Method overloading: Method overloading is in the same class , where more than one method have the same name but different signatures
Ex


```
void sum (int a , int b);
void sum (int a , int b, int c);
void sum (float a, double b);
```

Method overriding : Method overriding is when one of the **methods** in the **super class** is **redefined** in the **sub-class**. In this case the signature of the method remains the same.
Ex

```
class X{
 public int sum(){
   // some code
 }
}

class Y extends X{
 public int sum(){
  //overridden method
  //signature is same
```

}
}

Difference between static & Dynamic polymorphism

Static Polymorphism : It relates to method overloading .Errors ,if any, are resolved at compile time. Since the code is not executed during execution , the name static.

Ex:

```
void sum (int a , int b);
void sum (float a, double b);
int sum (int a, int b); //compiler gives error.
```

Dynamic Polymorphism: It relates to method overriding.

In case a reference variable is calling an overridden method, the method to be invoked is determined by the object ,your reference variable is pointing to. This is can be only determined at run -time when code in under execution , hence the name dynamic.

Chapter 6: Memory

Java Stack and Heap

The JVM divided the memory into following sections.

1. Heap

2. Stack

3. Code

4. Static

This division of memory is required for its effective management.

- The **code** section contains your **bytecode**.

- The **Stack** section of memory contains **methods, local variables and reference variables.**

- The **Heap** section contains **Objects** (may also contain reference variables).

- The **Static** section contains **Static data/methods.**

Of all of the above 4 sections, you need to understand the allocation of memory in Stack & Heap the most, since it will affect your programming efforts.

Difference between Local and instance variable

Instance variable are declared **inside a class but not inside a method**

```
class Student{
int num; // num is  instance variable
public void showData{}
```

Local variable are declared **inside** a **method including** method **arguments.**

```
public void sum(int a){

int x = int a +  3;

// a , x are local variables</strong>

}
```

Let's take an example to understand this better.

Consider that your main method calling method m1

```
public void m1{
int x=20
}
```

In the stack java, a frame will be created from method m1.

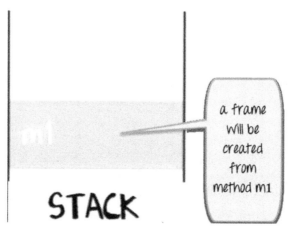

The variable X in m1 will also be created in the frame for m1 in the stack. (See image below).

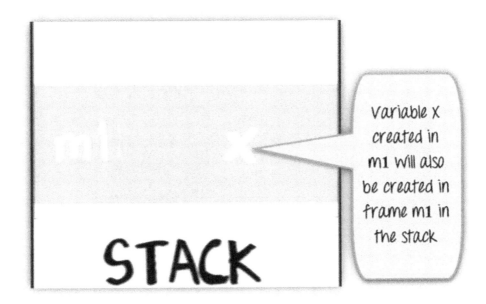

Method m1 is calling method m2. In the stack java, a new frame is created for m2 on top of the frame m1.

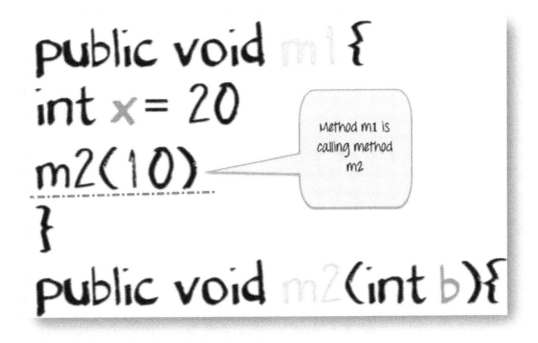

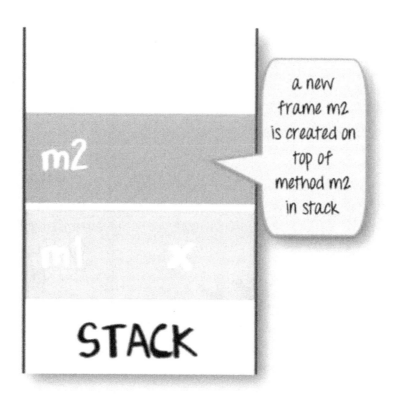

Variable b and c will also be created in a frame m2 in a stack.

```
public void m2(int b){
boolean c;
}
```

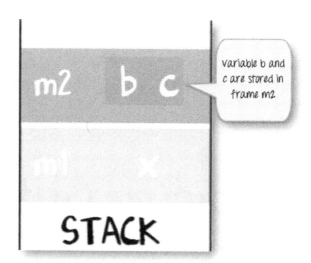

Same method m2 is calling method m3. Again a frame m3 is created on the top of the stack (see image below).

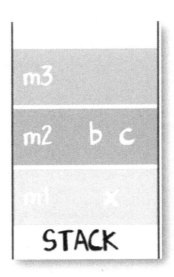

```
public void m2(int b){
    boolean c;
    //more code
    m3();
}
```

> another method m3 is called by method m2

```
public void m3()
```

Now let say our method m3 is creating an object for class "Account," which has two instances variable int p and int q.

```
Account {
        Int p;
        Int q;
    }
```

Here is the code for m3

```
public void m3(){
    Account ref = new Account();
```

```
        // more code
}
```

The statement new Account() will create an object of account in heap.

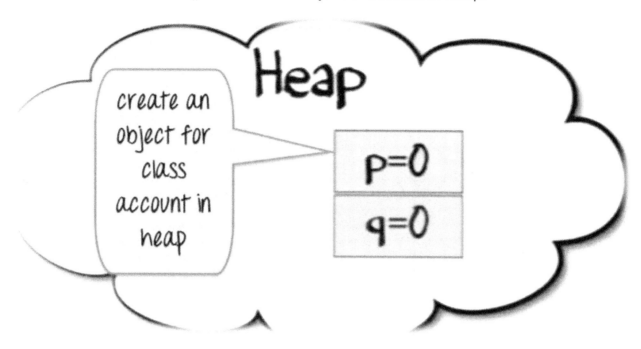

The reference variable "ref" will be created in a stack java.

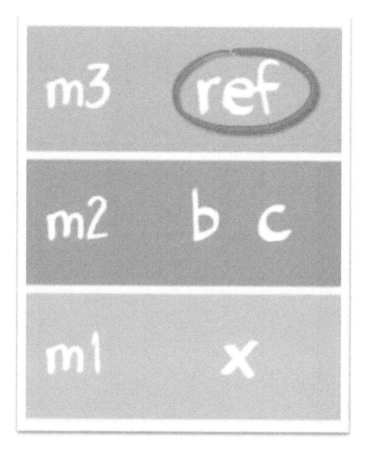

The assign "=" operator will make a reference variable to point to the object in the Heap.

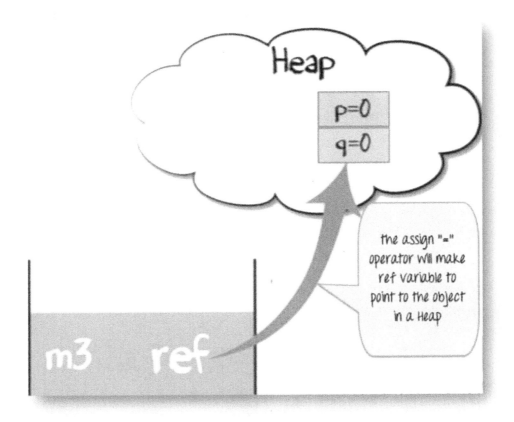

Once the method has completed its execution. The flow of control will go back to the calling method. Which in this case is m2.

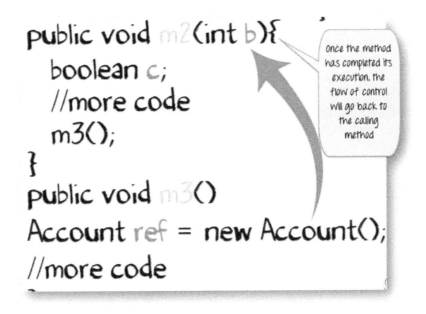

The stack from method m3 will be flushed out.

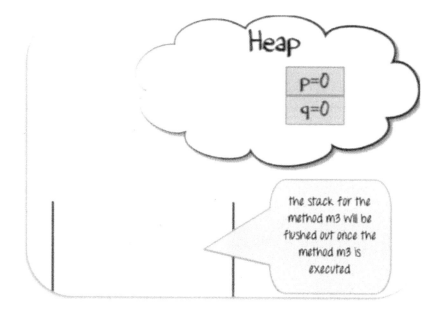

Since the reference variable will no longer be pointing to the object in the heap, it would be eligible for garbage collection.

Once m2 has completed its execution. It will be poped out of the stack, and all its variable will be flushed and no longer be available for use.

Likewise for method m1.

Eventually, the flow of control will return to the startpoint of the program. Which usually, is the "main" method.

Summary:

- When a method is called , a frame is created on the top of stack.

- Once a method has completed execution , flow of control returns to the calling method and its corresponding stack frame is flushed.

- Local variables are created in the stack

- Instance variables are created in the heap & are part of the object they belong to.

- Reference variables are created in the stack.

Point to Ponder: What if Object has a reference as its instance variable?

public static void main(String args[]){ A parent = new A(); //more code } class A{ B child = new B(); int e; //more code } class B{ int c; int d; //more code }

In this case , the reference variable "child" will be created in heap ,which in turn will be pointing to its object, something like the diagram shown below.

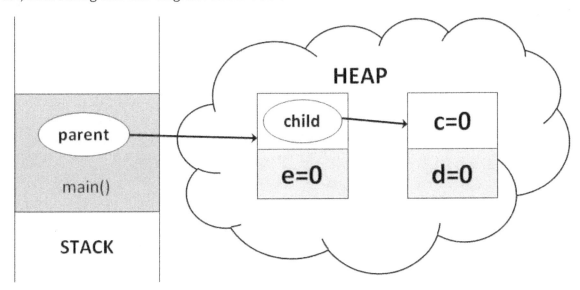

Java Static Methods and Variables

Typres of Variable

1. static variables

2. static methods

3. static blocks of code.

Lets look at static variables and static methods first.

Java static variable

- It is a variable which **belongs to the class** and **not** to **object**(instance)

- Static variables are **initialized only once** , at the start of the execution . These variables will be initialized first, before the initialization of any instance variables

- A **single copy** to be shared by all instances of the class

- A static variable can be **accessed directly** by the **class name** and doesn't need any object

- Syntax : **<CLASS-NAME>.<VARIABLE-NAME>**

Java Static Method

- It is a method which **belongs to the class** and **not** to the **object**(instance)

- A static method **can access only static data**. It can not access non-static data (instance variables)

- A static method **can call only** other **static methods** and can not call a non-static method from it.

- A static method can be **accessed directly** by the **class name** and doesn't need any object

- Syntax : **<CLASS-NAME>.<METHOD-NAME>**

- A static method cannot refer to "this" or "super" keywords in anyway

Side Note:

- main method is static , since it must be be accessible for an application to run , before any instantiation takes place.

LETS LEARN THE NUANCES OF THE STATIC KEYWORDS BY DOING SOME EXCERCISES!

Assignment: To Learn working of static variables & methods

Step 1) Copy the following code into a editor

```
public class Demo{
   public static void main(String args[]){
     Student s1 = new Student();
     s1.showData();
     Student s2 = new Student();
     s2.showData();
     //Student.b++;
     //s1.showData();
   }
}
```

```java
class Student {
int a; //initialized to zero
static int b; //initialized to zero only when class is loaded not for each object created.

  Student(){
   //Constructor incrementing static variable b
   b++;
  }

  public void showData(){
      System.out.println("Value of a = "+a);
      System.out.println("Value of b = "+b);
   }
//public static void increment(){
//a++;
//}


}
```

Step 2) Save & Compile the code. Run the code as, **java Demo**.

Step 3) Expected output show below

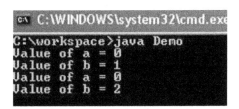

Following diagram shows , how reference variables & objects are created and static variables are accessed by the different instances.

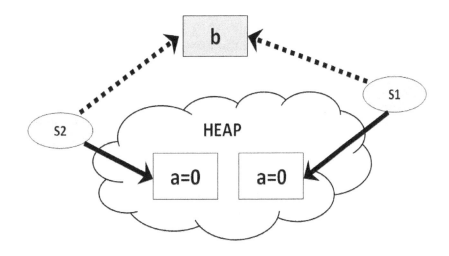

Step 4) It is possible to access a static variable from outside the class using the syntax **ClassName.Variable_Name**. Uncomment line # 7 & 8 . Save , Compile & Run . Observe the output.

Step 5) Uncomment line 25,26 & 27 . Save , Compile & Run.

Step 6) Error = ? This is because it is not possible to access instance variable "**a**" from java static class method "**increment**".

STATIC BLOCK

The static block, is a block of statement inside a Java class that will be executed when a class is first loaded in to the JVM

```
class Test{
 static {
 //Code goes here
 }
 }
```

A **static block helps to initialize the static data members**, just like constructors help to initialize instance members

How "Garbage Collection" Works in Java?

What is Garbage Collection

In the Java programming language, dynamic allocation of objects is achieved using the **new** operator. An object once created uses some memory and the memory remains allocated till there are references for the use of the object.

When there are no references for an object, it is assumed to be no longer needed and the memory occupied by the object can be reclaimed. There is no explicit need to destroy an object as java handles the de-allocation automatically.

The technique that accomplishes this is known as **Garbage Collection**. Programs that do not de-allocate memory can eventually crash when there is no memory left in the system to allocate. These programs are said to have memory leaks

Garbage collection in java happens automatically during the lifetime of a java program, eliminating the need to de-allocate memory and avoiding memory leaks.

In C language, it is the programmer's responsibility to de-allocate memory allocated dynamically using free() function. This is where Java memory management leads.

Note : All objects are created in **Heap** Section of memory. More on this in a later tutorial.

Assignment: To Learn Garbage Collector Mechanism in Java

Step 1) Copy the following code into a editor

```
class Student{
int a;
int b;

  public void setData(int c,int d){
    a=c;
    b=d;
  }
  public void showData(){
    System.out.println("Value of a = "+a);
    System.out.println("Value of b = "+b);
  }
  public static void main(String args[]){
    Student s1 = new Student();
    Student s2 = new Student();
    s1.setData(1,2);
    s2.setData(3,4);
    s1.showData();
    s2.showData();
    //Student s3;
    //s3=s2;
    //s3.showData();
    //s2=null;
    //s3.showData();
    //s3=null;
    //s3.showData();
  }
}
```

Step 2) Save, Compile and Run the code. As shown in the diagram , two objects and two reference variables are created.

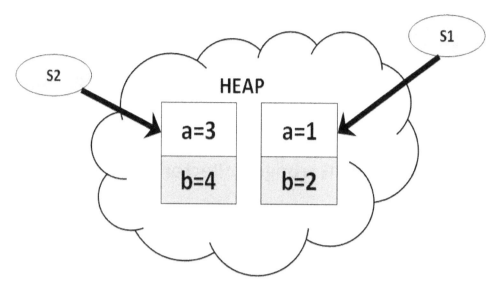

Step 3) Uncomment line # 20,21,22. Save , compile & run the code.

Step 4) As show in diagram below, two reference variables are pointing to the same object.

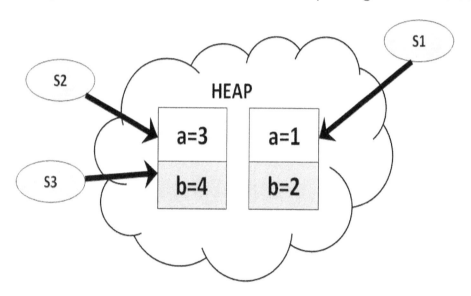

Step 5) Uncomment line # 23 & 24. Compile , Save & Run the code

Step 6) As show in diagram below , s2 becomes null , but s3 is still pointing to the object and is not eligible for java garbage collection.

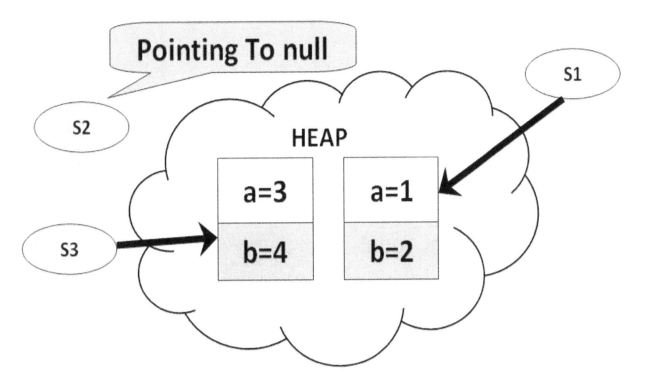

Step 7) Uncomment line # 25 & 26 . Save , Compile & Run the Code

Step 8) At this point there are no references pointing to the object and becomes eligible for garbage collection. It will be removed from memory and there is no way of retrieving it back.

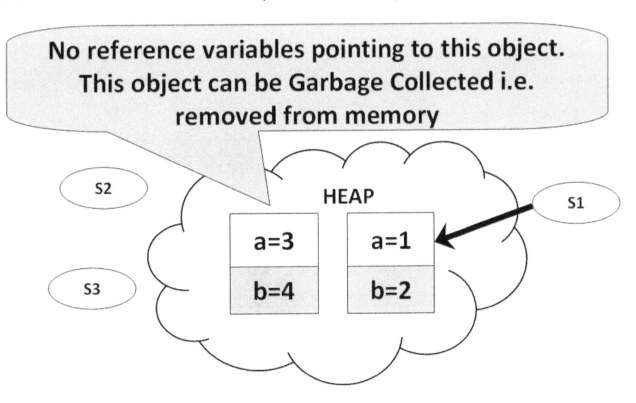

Garbage Collection Important Points to Note:

1) If you want to make your object eligible for Garbage Collection , assign its reference variable to null.

2) Primitive types are not objects. They cannot be assigned null.

Chapter :7 Conditional Loops

How to Loop/Iterate an array in Java

Let us take the example using a String array that you want to iterate over without using any counters.

Consider a String array arrData initialized as follows:

```
String[] arrData = {"Alpha", "Beta", "Gamma", "Delta", "Sigma"};
```

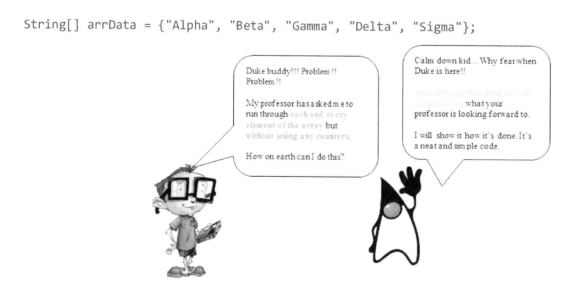

Although, you might know methods like finding the size of the array and then iterating through each element of the array using the traditional for loop (counter, condition and increment), we need to find a more optimized approach that will not use any such counter.

This is the conventional approach of the "for" loop:

```
for(int i = 0; i< arrData.length; i++){

System.out.println(arrData[i]);

}
```

You can see the use of the counter and then using it as the index for the array.

Java provides a way to use the "for" loop that will iterate through each element of the array as shown below.

Following will be the syntactical template:

```
For(<DataType of array/List><Temp variable name>   : <Array/List to be iterated>){
   System.out.println();
//Any other operation can be done with this temp variable.
}
```

Here is the code for the array that we had declared earlier-

```
for (String strTemp : arrData){

System.out.println(strTemp);

}
```

You can see the difference between the loops. The *code* has *reduced* significantly. Also there is *no use of the index* or rather the *counter in the loop*.

Do ensure that, the *data type* declared in the foreach loop *must match* the data type of the *array/list that you are iterating*.
Here we have the entire class showing the above explanation-

```
class UsingForEach {
 public static void main(String[] args) {
   String[] arrData = {"Alpha", "Beta", "Gamma", "Delta", "Sigma"};
   //The conventional approach of using the for loop
   System.out.println("Using conventional For Loop:");
   for(int i=0; i< arrData.length; i++){
     System.out.println(arrData[i]);
   }
   System.out.println("\nUsing Foreach loop:");
   //The optimized method of using the for loop - also called the foreach loop
```

```
   for (String strTemp : arrData){
     System.out.println(strTemp);
    }
  }
}
```

Java Switch Case Tutorial

We all use switches regularly in our lives. Yes, I am talking about electrical switches we use for our lights and fans.

As you see from the below picture, each switch is assigned to operate for particular electrical equipment.

For example, in the picture, the first switch is for fan, next for light and so on.

Thus, we can see that each switch can activate/deactivate only 1 item.

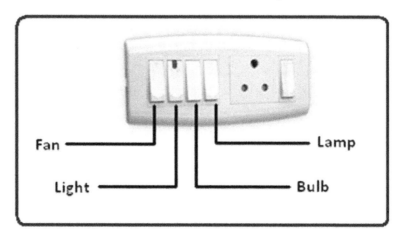

What is Switch Case in Java?

Similarly, switch in java is a type of conditional statement that activates only the matching condition out of the given input.

Let us consider the example of a program where the user gives input as a numeric value (only 1 digit in this example) and the output should be the number in words.

The integer variable iSwitch ,is the input for the switch to work.

The various available options (read cases) are then written as case <value>alongwith a colon ":"

This will then have the statement to be executed if the case and the input to the switch match.

Java Switch Example

```java
class SwitchBoard{
 public static void main(String args[]){
   int iSwitch=4;
   switch(iSwitch){
     case 0:
     System.out.println("ZERO");
     break;

     case 1:
     System.out.println("ONE");
     break;

     case 2:
     System.out.println("TWO");
     break;

     case 3:
     System.out.println("THREE");
     break;

     case 4:
     System.out.println("FOUR");
     break;

     default:
     System.out.println("Not in the list");
     break;
 }
}
```

```
}
```

Now what are those 2 words break and default lying out there do?

- The first one "break" – will simply break out from the switch block once a condition is satisfied.

- "Default" – This will be executed in case none of the conditions match the given input.

In the given example these are simple print statements, however they can also refer to more complex situations like calling a method etc.

What if you do not provide a break?

In case the break is not provided, it will execute the matching conditions as well as the default condition. Your logic will go haywire if that occurs.

I will leave it to the users to experiment without using break.

Java Switch statement:

- As a standard programming logic, it can simply be achieved by using if...else conditions, but then it will not be optimized for good programming practicenor does the code look readable.

- In programs involving more complex cases, scenarios will not be so simple and would require calling several methods.Switch solves this problem and avoids several nested if...else statements.Also, while using if....else, it is recommended to use the most highly expected condition to be on top and then go ahead in a nested manner.

- SOME BENCHMARKING TESTS HAVE PROVEN THAT IN JAVA CASE OF HIGH NUMBER OF ITERATIONS, THE SWITCH IS FASTER AS COMPARED TO IF....ELSE STATEMENTS.

Points to Note

- There is no limit on the number of case java you can have.

- Switch java can take input only as integers or characters.

- The latest version of Java8, also introduces the much awaited support for java switch strings statement.

So now go ahead and wire your own switch board!!

Chapter 8 Exception Handling

Java Exception Handling

Disruption during the execution of the program is referred as error or exception. In other words, an exception is any event that interrupts the normal flow of execution.

There are two types of errors,

- Compile time errors
- Runtime errors

Compile time errors can be again classified again into two types.

Compile time error	Run time error

- Syntax Errors
 	
  Example: Integer **Int a;**
 	
  you mistakenly declared it as
 	
  in a;
 	
  for which compiler will throw an error.
	- A Runtime error is called an **Exceptions** error. It is any event that interrupts the normal flow of program execution.
	
	  Example for exceptions are, arithmetic exception, Nullpointer exception, Divide by zero exception, etc.
	
	  Exceptions in java are something that are out of developers control.

- Semantic Errors

  Example: You have
  declared a variable (int
  a;) and after some lines
  of code you again
  declare an integer as (int
  a;). All these errors are
  highlighted when you
  compile teh code.

Suppose you have coded a program to access the server. Things worked fine while you were developing the code.

Please be patient. The Video will load in some time. If you still face issue viewing video click **here**

During the actual production run, the server is down. When your program tried to access it, an exception is raised.

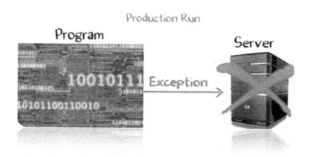

How to handle exception

So far we have seen what exception is.

But blaming your code failure on environmental issues is not a solution. You need a Robust Programming, which takes care of exceptional situations. Such code is known as **Exception Handler.**

In our example, good exception handling would be, when the server is down connect to the backup server.

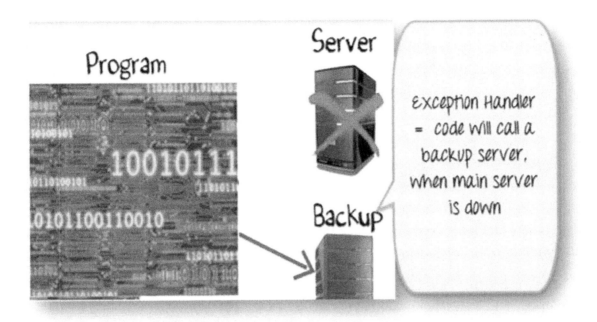

To implement this, enter your code to connect to the server (Using traditional if and else conditions).

You will check if the server is down.

If yes write the code to connect to the backup server.

Such organization of code, using "if" and "else" loop is not effective when your code has multiple java exceptions to handle.

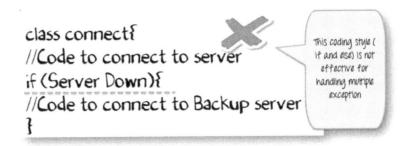

Hence, Java provides an inbuilt exceptional handling.

1. The normal code goes into **TRY** block.

2. The exception handling code goes into the **CATCH** block

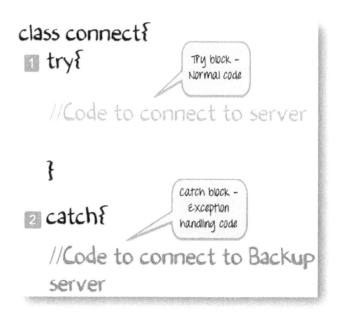

In our example, TRY block will contain the code to connect to the server. CATCH block will contain the code to connect to the backup server.

In case the server is up, the code in the CATCH block will be ignored. In case the server is down, an exception is raised, and the code in catch block will be executed.

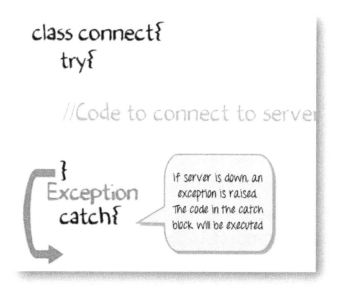

So, this is how the exception is handled in Java.

A Summary of the points covered in the above demonstration –

1. An **Exception is a run-time error** which interrupts the normal flow of program execution.

2. A **robust program should handle all exceptions** and continue with its normal flow of program execution.

3. **Exception Handler** is a set of code that **handles an exception**.

Exceptions can be handled in Java using **try & catch**.

Sytanx for using try & catch

```
try{
    statement(s)
    }
    catch (exceptiontype name){
    statement(s)
    }
```

Step 1) Copy the following code into an editor

```
class JavaException {
  public static void main(String args[]){
    int d = 0;
    int n =20;
    int fraction = n/d;
    System.out.println("End Of Main");
  }
}
```

Step 2) Save the file & compile the code. Run the program using command, **java JavaException**.

Step 3) An Arithmetic Exception - divide by zero is shown as below for line # 5 and line # 6 is never executed**.**

Step 4) Now lets see examine how try and catch will help us handle this exception. We will put the exception causing line of code into a **try** block , followed by a **catch** block. Copy the following code into editor.

```
class JavaException {
        public static void main(String args[]){
                int d = 0;
                int n =20;
        try{
                int fraction = n/d;
                System.out.println("This line will not be Executed");
                }
        catch(ArithmeticException e){
                System.out.println("In the catch Block due to Exception = "+e);
                }
        System.out.println("End Of Main");
        }
}
```

Step 5) Save , Compile & Run the code.You will get the following output

```
C:\workspace>java JavaException
In the catch clock due to Exception = java.lang.ArithmeticException: / by zero
End Of Main
```

As you observe , the exception is handled and the last line of code is also executed. Also note that Line # 7 will not be executed because **as soon as an exception is raised flow of control jumps to the catch block .**

Note: The AritmeticException Object "e" carries information about the exception that has occurred which can be useful in taking recovery actions.

Java Finally Block

The finally block is **executed irrespective of an exception being raised** in the try block.It is **optional** to use with a try block.

```
try{

    statement(s)
    }


    catch(ExceptiontType name){

    statement(s)


    }


    finally{

    statement(s)


    }
```

In case, an exception is raised in the try block, finally block is executed after the catch block is executed.

Assignment

Step 1) Copy the following code into an editor.

```java
class JavaException {
    public static void main(String args[]){
      try{
        int d = 0;
        int n =20;
        int fraction = n/d;
```

```
    }
  catch(ArithmeticException e){
    System.out.println("In the catch clock due to Exception = "+e);
  }
  finally{
  System.out.println("Inside the finally block");
  }
}
}
```

Step 2) Save , Compile & Run the Code.

Step 3) Expected output. Finally block is executed even though an exception is raised.

Step 4) Change the value of variable d = 1 . Save , Compile and Run the code and observe the output.Bottom of Form

Summary:

- Disruption during the execution of the program is referred as error or exception.

- Errors are classified into two categories

    o   Compile time errors – Syntax errors, Semantic errors

    o   Runtime errors- Exception

- Java provides an inbuilt exceptional handling method

- **Try block**: Normal code goes into this block.

- **Catch block**: If there is error in normal code, then it will go into this block

Guide to Java Exception Hierarchy

In case there are multiple exceptions that might arise in a try block, you can provide several catch blocks each handling a different type of exception.

Try Catch Syntax:-

```
try{
statement(s)
}
catch (exceptiontype name){
}
```

```
catch (exceptiontype name){
}
catch (exceptiontype name){
}
catch (exceptiontype name){
}
```

Java Exception class Hierachy

After one catch statement executes, the others are bypassed, and execution continues after the try/catch block. The nested catch blocks follow Exception hierarchy.

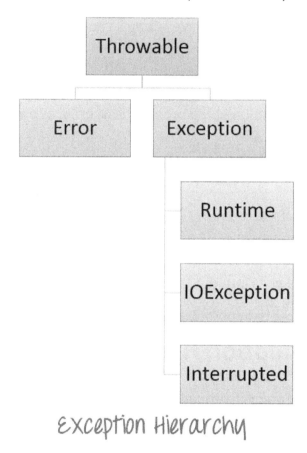

Exception Hierarchy

- All exception classes in java extends the class 'Throwable'. 'Throwable' has two sub classes, Error and Exception

- The Error class defines the exception or the problems that are not expected to be occur under normal circumstances by our program, example Memory error, Hardware error , JVM error etc

- • The Exception class represents the exceptions that can be handled by our program and our program can be recovered from this exception using try and catch block

- Runtime exception is a sub-class of the exception class. Exception of these type represents exception that occur at the run time and which cannot be track at the compile time. A very good example of same is divide by zero exception, or null pointer exception etc

- IO exception is generated during input and output operations

- Interrupted exceptions in java, is generated during multiple threading.

Assignment: To understand nesting of try and catch blocks

Step 1) Copy the following code into an editor

```
class JavaException {
        public static void main(String args[]){
        try{
                int d =1;
                int n =20;
                int fraction = n/d;
                int g[] ={1} ;
                g[20] =100;
                }
        /*catch(Exception e){
                System.out.println("In the catch clock due to Exception = "+e);
        }*/
        catch(ArithmeticException e){
                System.out.println("In the catch clock due to Exception = "+e);
        }
        catch(ArrayIndexOutOfBoundsException e){
                System.out.println("In the catch clock due to Exception = "+e);
        }
                System.out.println("End Of Main");
        }
}
```

Step 2) Save the file & compile the code. Run the program using command, **java JavaException**.

Step 3) An ArrayIndexOutOfBoundsException is generated. Change the value of int d to 0. Save ,Compile & Run the code.

Step 4) An ArithmeticException must be generated.

Step 5) Uncomment line #10 to line #12 . Save , Compile & Run the code.

Step 6) **Compilation Errror ?** This is because Exception is the base class of ArithmeticException

Exception. Any Exception that is raised by ArithmeticException can be handled by Exception class as well .So the catch block of ArithmeticException will never get a chance to be executed which makes it redundant. Hence the compilation error.

Create User Defined Exception in Java

More often than not, in your programming projects, you will be required to define **java custom Exceptions also called User-defined Exceptions**. This can be done by extending the class Exception.

Exception

getLocalizedMessage()
getMessage()
toString()

There is no need to override any of the above methods available in the Exception class ,in your derived class. But practically, you will require some amount of customizing as per your programming needs.

Assignment: To created a User Defined Exception Class

Step 1) Copy the following code into the editor

```
class JavaException{
   public static void main(String args[]){
  try{
       throw new MyException(2);
       // throw is used to create a new exception and throw it.
  }
 catch(MyException e){
    System.out.println(e) ;
 }
}
}
```

```
}
class MyException extends Exception{
   int a;
   MyException(int b) {
     a=b;
   }
   public String toString(){
      return ("Exception Number =   "+a) ;
   }
}
```

Step 2) Save , Compile & Run the code. Excepted output -

NOTE:

The keyword **"throw"** is used to create a new Exception and throw it to the catch block.

How to use "throws" keyword in Java Exception

Suppose in your java program you using a library method which throws an Exception

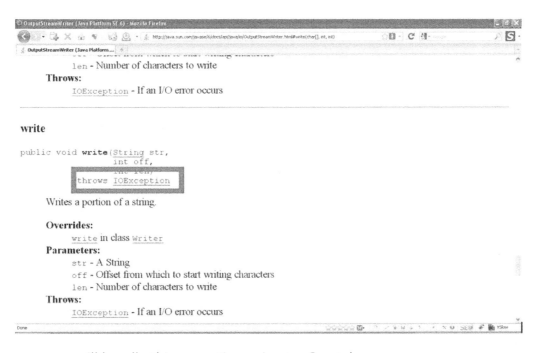

In your program you will handle this exception using try & catch.

```
import java.io.*;
class file1{
```

```java
    public static void main(String[] args) {
        try{
                FileWriter file = new FileWriter("c:\\Data1.txt");
                file.write("Guru99");
                file.close();
        }
        catch(IOException){}
    }
}
```

If you do not handle the exception in a try catch block, compiling will fail. But almost every other method in the java library or even user defined may throw an exception or two.

Handling all the exceptions using the try and catch block could be cumbersome and will hinder the coders throughput.

So java provides an option, wherein whenever you are using a risky piece of code in the method definition you declare it **throws** an exception without implementing try catch.

Syntax of java throw Exception

```java
method (Arguments) throws Exception1,Exception2,Exception,… {}
```

Java throws example

Consider the same example as above with throws in method declaration.

```java
import java.io.*;
class file1{
    public static void main(String[] args) throws IOException{
        FileWriter file = new FileWriter("c:\\Data1.txt");
        file.write("Guru99");
        file.close();
    }
}
```

Note: To successfully the above codes , first create an empty text file with name Data1.txt in your C drive. In sum, there are two methods to handle Exceptions.

1. Put the Exception causing code in try and catch block.

2. Declare the method to be throwing an Exception

If either of the above two is not done, compiler gives an error. **The idea behind enforcing this rule is that you as a programmer are aware that a certain piece of code could be risky and may throw an exception.**

What is the difference between throw and throws?

throw : It is used to create a new Exception object and throw it
throws : is used in method definition , to declare that a risky method is being called.

Summary

The **"Java throw keyword"** is used to declare an exception. For any method that will "throw" an exception, it is mandatory that in the calling method, you use throws to list the exception thrown.

Chapter 9 Math

Java has had several advanced usage application including working with complex calculations in physics, architecture/designing of structures, working with Maps and corresponding latitudes/longitudes etc.

All such applications require using complex calculations/equations that are tedious to perform manually. Programmatically, such calculations, would involve usage of logarithms, trigonometry, exponential equations etc.

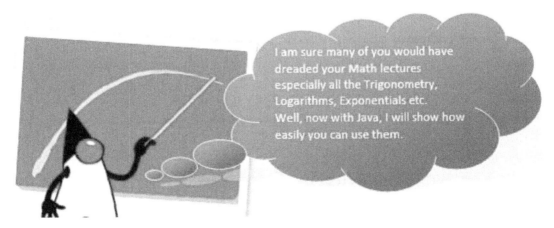

Now, you cannot have all the log or trigonometry tables hard-coded somewhere in your application or data. The data would be enormous and complex to maintain.

Java provides a very useful class for this purpose. It is the Math java class (java.lang.Math).

This class provides methods for performing the operations like exponential, logarithm, roots and trigonometric equations too.

Let us have a look at the methods provided by the Java Math class.

The 2 most fundamental elements in Math are the 'e' (base of the natural logarithm) and 'pi' (ratio of the circumference of a circle to its diameter). These 2 constants are often required in the above calculations/operations.

Hence the Math class java provides these 2 constants as double fields.

Math.E - having a value as **2.718281828459045**

Math.PI - having a value as **3.141592653589793**

A) Let us have a look at the table below that shows us the **Basic methods** and its description

Method	Description	Arguments
abs	Returns the absolute value of the argument	Double, float, int, long
round	Returns the closed int or long (as per the argument)	double or float
ceil	Returns the smallest integer that is greater than or equal to the argument	Double
floor	Returns the largest integer that is less than or equal to the argument	Double
min	Returns the smallest of the two arguments	Double, float, int, long
max	Returns the largest of the two arguments	Double, float, int, long

Below is the code implementation for the above methods:

Note: There is no need to explicitly import java.lang.Math as its imported implicitly. All its methods are static

Integer Variable

```
int i1 = 27;
int i2 = -45;
```

Double(decimal) variables

```
double d1 = 84.6;
double d2 = 0.45;
```

Math.abs

```
System.out.println("Absolute value of i1: " + Math.abs(i1));
Absolute value of i1: 27


System.out.println("Absolute value of i2: " + Math.abs(i2));
Absolute value of i2: 45


System.out.println("Absolute value of d1: " + Math.abs(d1));
Absolute value of d1: 84.6


System.out.println("Absolute value of d2: " + Math.abs(d2));
Absolute value of d2: 0.45
```

Math.round

```
System.out.println("Round off for d1: " + Math.round java(d1));
Round off for d1: 85


System.out.println("Round off for d2: " + Math.round java(d2));
Round off for d2: 0
```

Math.ceil & Math.floor

```
System.out.println("Ceiling of '"+ d1 + "' = " + Math.ceil(d1));
Ceiling of '84.6' = 85.0


System.out.println("Floor of '"+ d1 + "' = " + Math.floor(d1));
Floor of '84.6' = 84.0


System.out.println("Ceiling of '"+ d2 + "' = " + Math.ceil(d2));
Ceiling of '0.45' = 1.0
```

```
System.out.println("Floor of '"+ d2 + "' = " + Math.floor(d2));
Floor of '0.45' = 0.0
```

Math.min

```
System.out.println("Minimum out of '"+ i1 +"' and '" + i2+"' = "+ Math.min(i1, i2));
Minimum out of '27' and '-45' = -45
```

```
System.out.println("Maximum out of '"+ i1 +"' and '" + i2+"' = "+ Math.max(i1, i2));
Maximum out of '27' and '-45' = 27
```

```
System.out.println("Minimum out of '"+ d1 +"' and '" + d2+"' = "+ Math.min(d1, d2));
Minimum out of '84.6' and '0.45' = 0.45
```

```
System.out.println("Maximum out of '"+ d1 +"' and '" + d2+"' = "+ Math.max(d1, d2));
Maximum out of '84.6' and '0.45' = 84.6
```

B) Let us have a look at the table below that shows us the **Exponential and Logarithmic methods** and its description-

Method	Description	Arguments
exp	Returns the base of natural log (e) to the power of argument	Double
Log	Returns the natural log of the argument	double
Pow	Takes 2 arguments as input and returns the value of the first argument raised to the power of the second argument	Double
floor	Returns the largest integer that is less than or equal to the argument	Double
Sqrt	Returns the square root of the argument	Double

Below is the code implementation for the above methods: (The same variables are used as above)

```
System.out.println("exp(" + d2 + ") = " + Math.exp(d2));
exp(0.45) = 1.5683121854901687
```

```
System.out.println("log(" + d2 + ") = " + Math.log(d2));
```

```
log(0.45) = -0.7985076962177716
```

```
System.out.println("pow(5, 3) = " + Math.pow(5.0, 3.0));
pow(5, 3) = 125.0
```

```
System.out.println("sqrt(16) = " + Math.sqrt(16));
sqrt(16) = 4.0
```

C) Let us have a look at the table below that shows us the **Trigonometric methods** and its description-

Method	Description	Arguments
Sin	Returns the Sine of the specified argument	Double
Cos	Returns the Cosine of the specified argument	double
Tan	Returns the Tangent of the specified argument	Double
Atan2	Converts rectangular co-ordinates (x, y) to polar(r, theta) and returns theta	Double
toDegrees	Converts the arguments to degrees	Double
Sqrt	Returns the square root of the argument	Double
toRadians	Converts the arguments to radians	Double

Default Arguments are in Radians

Below is the code implementation:

```
double angle_30 = 30.0;
double radian_30 = Math.toRadians(angle_30);
```

```
System.out.println("sin(30) = " + Math.sin(radian_30));
sin(30) = 0.49999999999999994
```

```
System.out.println("cos(30) = " + Math.cos(radian_30));
cos(30) = 0.8660254037844387
```

```
System.out.println("tan(30) = " + Math.tan(radian_30));
tan(30) = 0.5773502691896257


System.out.println("Theta = " + Math.atan2(4, 2));
Theta = 1.1071487177940904
```

Now, with the above, you can also design your own scientific calculator in java.

Generating Random Number Using Java

Well, Java does provide some interesting ways to generate java random numbers, not only for gambling but also several other applications esp. related to gaming, **security**, math's etc.

Let's see how it's done!!There are basically two ways to do it-

- o Using Randomclass (in package java.util).

- o Using Math.random java class (however this will generate double in the range of 0.0 to 1.0 and not integers).

Lets look at them one by one -

Example: Using Java Random Class

First we will see the implementation using java.util.Random-Assume we need to generate 10 random numbers between 0 to 100.

```
import java.util.Random;
public class RandomNumbers{
      public static void main(String[] args) {
        Random objGenerator = new Random();
          for (int iCount = 0; iCount< 10; iCount++){
            int randomNumber = objGenerator.nextInt(100);
            System.out.println("Random No : " + randomNumber);
            }
      }
}
```

An object of Random class is initialized as objGenerator. The Random class has a method as nextInt. This will provide a random number based on the argument specified as the upper limit, whereas it takes lower limit is 0.Thus, we get 10 random numbers displayed.

Example: Using Java Math.Random

Now, if we want 10random numbers generated java but in the range of 0.0 to 1.0, then we should make use of math.random()

You can use the following loop to generate them-

```
public class DemoRandom{
  public static void main(String[] args) {
    for(int xCount = 0; xCount< 10; xCount++){
      System.out.println(Math.random());
    }
  }
}
```

Now, you know how those strange numbers are generated!!!

Chapter 10 Important Stuff

Any application can have multiple process (instances). Each of this process can be assigned either as a single thread or multiple threads.

- **Single Thread**: A single thread is basically a lightweight and the smallest unit of processing.

- **Multi-Thread**: While multithreading can be defined as the execution of two or more threads concurrently.

We will see in this tutorial how to perform multiple tasks at the same time and also learn more about threads and synchronization between threads.

What is Single Thread and Multithread

Threads

As we have discussed earlier, a single thread is the smallest unit of processing. Java uses threads by using a "Thread Class".

There are two types of thread – **user thread and daemon thread** (daemon threads are used when we want to clean the application and are used in the background).

When an application first begins, user thread is created. Post that, we can create many user threads and daemon threads.

Single Thread Example:

```
package demotest;
```

```java
public class GuruThread1 implements Runnable
{

    /**
     * @param args
     */
    public static void main(String[] args) {
        Thread guruThread1 = new Thread("Guru1");
        Thread guruThread2 = new Thread("Guru2");
        guruThread1.start();
        guruThread2.start();
        System.out.println("Thread names are following:");
        System.out.println(guruThread1.getName());
        System.out.println(guruThread2.getName());
    }
    @Override
    public void run() {
    }

}
```

Advantages of single thread:

- Reduces overhead in the application as single thread execute in the system

- Also, it reduces the maintenance cost of the application.

Multithreads

Multithreaded applications are where two or more threads run concurrently. This multitasking is done, when multiple process shares common resources like CPU, memory, etc.

Each thread runs parallel to each other. Threads don't allocate separate memory area, hence it saves memory. Also, context switching between threads takes less time.

Example of Multi thread:

```java
package demotest;
public class GuruMultithread implements Runnable{

    /**
     * @param args
     */
    public static void main(String[] args) {
            Thread guruthread1 = new Thread();
            guruthread1.start();
            Thread guruthread2 = new Thread();
```

```
        guruthread2.start();
    }

    @Override
    public void run() {
        // TODO Auto-generated method stub

    }

}
```

Advantages of multithread:

- The users are not blocked because threads are independent, and we can perform multiple operations at times

- As such the threads are independent, the other threads won't get affected if one thread meets an exception.

Thread life cycle in java

Life cycle of a thread:

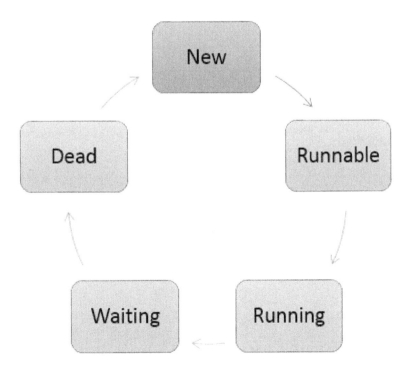

There are various stages in life cycle of thread as shown in above diagram:

1. New

2. Runnable

3. Running

4. Waiting

5. Dead

1. **New:** In this phase, the thread is created using class "Thread class".It remains in this state till the program **starts**the thread. It is also known as born thread.

2. **Runnable:** In this page, the instance of the thread is invoked with a start method. The thread control is given to scheduler to finish the execution. It depends on the scheduler, whether to run the thread.

3. **Running:** When the thread starts executing then the state is changed to "running" state. The scheduler selects one thread from the thread pool, and it starts executing in the application.

4. **Waiting:** This is the state when a thread has to wait. As there are multiple threads running in the application, there is a need for synchronization between threads. Hence, one thread has to wait, till the other thread get executed. Therefore, this state is referred as waiting state.

5. **Dead:** This is the state when the thread is terminated. The thread is in running state and as soon as it completed processing it is in "dead state".

Some of commonly used methods for threads are:

1. **start()**

   This method starts the execution of the thread and JVM calls the run() method on the thread.

   We will cover this in the below example.

2. **Sleep(int milliseconds)**

   This method makes the thread sleep hence the thread's execution will pause for milliseconds provided and after that, again the thread starts executing. This help in synchronization of the threads.

3. **getName():**

   It returns the name of the thread.

4. **setPriority(int newpriority)**

   It changes the priority of the thread.

5. **yield ()**

   It causes current thread on halt and other threads to execute.

Example: In this example we are going to create a thread and explore built-in methods available for threads.

```java
package demotest;
public class thread_example1 implements Runnable {
    @Override
    public void run() {
    }
    public static void main(String[] args) {
        Thread guruthread1 = new Thread();
        guruthread1.start();
        try {
            guruthread1.sleep(1000);
        } catch (InterruptedException e) {
            // TODO Auto-generated catch block
            e.printStackTrace();
        }
        guruthread1.setPriority(1);
        int gurupriority = guruthread1.getPriority();
        System.out.println(gurupriority);
        System.out.println("Thread Running");
    }
}
```

Explanation of the code:

Code Line 4: We are creating a class "thread_Example1" which is implementing the Runnable interface (it should be implemented by any class whose instances are intended to be executed by the thread.)

Code Line 7-8: It overrides run method of the runnable interface as it is mandatory to override that method

Code Line 9: Here we have defined the main method in which we will start the execution of the thread.

Code Line 10: Here we are creating a new thread name as "guruthread1" by instantiating a new class of thread.

Code Line 11: we will use "start" method of the thread using "guruthread1" instance. Here the thread will start executing.

Code Line 13: Here we are using the "sleep" method of the thread using "guruthread1" instance. Hence, the thread will sleep for 1000 milliseconds.

Code 12-17: Here we have put sleep method in try catch block as there is checked exception which occurs i.e. Interrupted exception.

Code Line 18: Here we are setting the priority of the thread to 1 from whichever priority it was

Code Line 19: Here we are getting the priority of the thread using getPriority()

Code Line 20: Here we are printing the value fetched from getPriority

Code Line 21: Here we are writing a text that thread is running.

When you execute the above code, you get the following output:

Output:

5 is the Thread priority, and Thread Running is the text which is the output of our code.

Java Thread Synchronization

In multithreading, there is the asynchronous behavior of the programs. If one thread is writing some data and another thread which is reading data at the same time, might create inconsistency in the application.

When there is a need to access the shared resources by two or more threads, then synchronization approach is utilized.

Java has provided synchronized methods to implement synchronized behavior.

In this approach, once the thread reaches inside the synchronized block, then no other thread can call that method on the same object. All threads have to wait till that thread finishes the synchronized block and comes out of that.

In this way, the synchronization helps in a multithreaded application. One thread has to wait till other thread finishes its execution only then the other threads are allowed for execution.

It can be written in the following form:

```
Synchronized(object)
{
    //Block of statements to be synchronized
}
```

Java multithreading example

In this example, we will take two threads and fetch the names of the thread.

Example1:

GuruThread1.java
package demotest;

```java
public class GuruThread1 implements Runnable{

  /**
   * @param args
   */
  public static void main(String[] args) {
    Thread guruThread1 = new Thread("Guru1");
    Thread guruThread2 = new Thread("Guru2");
    guruThread1.start();
    guruThread2.start();
    System.out.println("Thread names are following:");
    System.out.println(guruThread1.getName());
    System.out.println(guruThread2.getName());
  }
  @Override
  public void run() {
  }

}
```

Explanation of the code:

Code Line 3: We have taken a class "GuruThread1" which implements Runnable (it should be implemented by any class whose instances are intended to be executed by the thread.)

Code Line 8: This is the main method of the class

Code Line 9: Here we are instantiating the Thread class and creating an instance named as "guruThread1" and creating a thread.

Code Line 10: Here we are instantiating the Thread class and creating an instance named a "guruThread2" and creating a thread.

Code Line 11: We are starting the thread i.e. guruThread1.

Code Line 12: We are starting the thread i.e. guruThread2.

Code Line 13: Outputting the text as "Thread names are following:"

Code Line 14: Getting the name of thread 1 using method getName() of the thread class.

Code Line 15: Getting the name of thread 2 using method getName() of the thread class.

When you execute the above code, you get the following output:

```
Problems  Tasks  Properties  Servers  Data Source Explorer  Snippets  Console
<terminated> GuruThread1 [Java Application] C:\Program Files (x86)\Java\jre6\bin\javaw.exe (Mar 21, 2016 12:38:51 PM)
Thread names are following:
Guru1
Guru2
```

Output:

Thread names are being outputted here as

- Guru1

- Guru2

Example 2:

In this example, we will learn about overriding methods run() and start() method of a runnable interface and create two threads of that class and run them accordingly.

Also, we are taking two classes,

- One which will implement the runnable interface and

- Other one which will have the main method and execute accordingly.

```java
package demotest;
public class GuruThread2 {

  public static void main(String[] args) {
    // TODO Auto-generated method stub
    GuruThread3 threadguru1 = new GuruThread3("guru1");
    threadguru1.start();
    GuruThread3 threadguru2 = new GuruThread3("guru2");
    threadguru2.start();}
}
class GuruThread3 implements Runnable
{   Thread guruthread;
  private String guruname;
  GuruThread3(String name)
  {
    guruname = name;
  }
  @Override
  public void run() {
  System.out.println("Thread running" +guruname);
```

```
    for(int i=0;i<4;i++)
    {
        System.out.println(i);
        System.out.println(guruname);
        try {
            Thread.sleep(1000);
        } catch (InterruptedException e) {
            System.out.println("Thread has been interrupted");
        }
    }
    }
    public void start()
    {
        System.out.println("Thread started");
        if(guruthread==null)
        {
            guruthread = new Thread(this,guruname);
            guruthread.start();
        }

    }
}
```

Explanation of the code:

Code Line 3: Here we are taking a class "GuruThread2" which will have the main method in it.

Code Line 5: Here we are taking a main method of the class.

Code Line 7-8: Here we are creating an instance of class GuruThread3 (which is created in below lines of the code) as "threadguru1" and we are starting the thread.

Code Line 9-10: Here we are creating another instance of class GuruThread3 (which is created in below lines of the code) as "threadguru2" and we are starting the thread.

Code Line 12: Here we are creating a class "GuruThread3" which is implementing the runnable interface (it should be implemented by any class whose instances are intended to be executed by the thread.)

Code Line 13-14: we are taking two class variables from which one is of the type thread class and other of the string class.

Code Line 15-18: we are overriding the GuruThread3 constructor, which takes one argument as string type (which is threads name) that gets assigned to class variable guruname and hence the name of the thread is stored.

Code Line 20: Here we are overriding the run() method of the runnable interface.

Code Line 21: We are outputting the thread name using println statement.

Code Line 22-31: Here we are using a for loop with counter initialized to 0, and it should not be less than 4 (we can take any number hence here loop will run 4 times) and incrementing the counter. We are printing the thread name and also making the thread sleep for 1000 milliseconds within a try catch block as sleep method raised checked exception.

Code Line 33: Here we are overriding start method of the runnable interface.

Code Line 35: We are outputting the text "Thread started".

Code Line 36-40: Here we are taking an if condition to check whether class variable guruthread has value in it or no. If its null then we are creating an instance using thread class which takes the name as a parameter (value for which was assigned in the constructor). After which the thread is started using start() method.

When you execute the above code you get the following output:

Output:

There are two threads hence, we get two times message "Thread started".

We get the names of the thread as we have outputted them.

It goes into for loop where we are printing the counter and thread name and counter starts with 0.

The loop executes three times and in between the thread is slept for 1000 milliseconds.

Hence, first, we get guru1 then guru2 then again guru2 because the thread sleeps here for 1000 milliseconds and then next guru1 and again guru1, thread sleeps for 1000 milliseconds, so we get guru2 and then guru1.

Summary:

In this tutorial, we saw multithreaded applications in Java and how to use single and multithreads.

- In multithreading, users are not blocked as threads are independent and can perform multiple operations at time

- Various stages in life cycle of the thread are,

    o   New

    o   Runnable

    o   Running

    o   Waiting

    o   Dead

- We also learnt about synchronization between threads, which help the application to run smoothly.

- Multithreading makes many more application tasks easier.

How to use Date in Java

Let us first understand the parameters that consist of a **Date**.

It will primarily contain -

- The **year** (in either 2 or 4 digits)

- The **month** (in either 2 digits, First 3 letters of the month or the entire word of the month).

- The **date** (it will be the actual date of the month).

- The **day** (the day at the given date – like Sun, Mon, Tue etc).

In terms of computer systems, there are quite a lot of parameters that can be used to associate with a date. We shall see them in the later parts of this topic.

Displaying a Date in Java

Now let us see how Java provide us the **Date**, first we shall see how to get the **current date-**

Java provides a Date class under the **java.util package**, The package provides several methods to play around with the date.

You can use the Date object by invoking the **constructor of Date class** as follows:

```
import java.util.Date;
class Date_Ex1 {
 public static void main(String args[]) {
   // Instantiate a Date object by invoking its constructor
   Date objDate = new Date();
   // Display the Date & Time using toString()
   System.out.println(objDate.toString());
 }
}
```

Show the date in the specified format:

You all must have learnt the alphabets in your kindergarten ....

Let us now learn the ABC's of the date format.

G	y	M	d
Era Designator	Year in 4 digits	Month of the year	Day in a month
AD	2012	October or 10	25
h	H	m	s
Hour in AM/PM (12 hr)	Hour in 24 or	Minute in an hour	Second in minute
11	23	45	30
S	E	D	F
Millisecond	Day in a Week	Day in a year	Day of week in month
280	Saturday	277	2 (Second Sun in Oct)
w	W	a	k
Week in Year	Week in month	AM/PM Marker	Hour in a day
42	3	PM	23
K	z	'	''
Hour in AM/PM (0-11)	Time Zone	Escape for Text	Single Quote
09	Pacific Standard Time	Delimiter	

Don't worry, you don't need to remember all of these, they can be referred anytime you need to format a particular date.

How Dates Formats can be used?

Java provides a class called a SimpleDateFormat that allows you to format and parse dates in the as per your requirements.

You can use the above characters to specify the format-

For example:

1. Date format required: **2012.10.23 20:20:45 PST**

The appropriate date format specified will be- **yyyy.MM.dd HH:mm:ss zzz** 2 .

Date format required:**09:30:00 AM 23-May-2012**

The appropriate date format specified will be-**hh:mm:ss a dd-MMM-yyyy**

Tip: Be careful with the letter capitalization . If you mistake M with m , you will undesired results!

Lets learn this with a code example

```
import java.text.SimpleDateFormat;
import java.util.Date;
 class TestDates_Format {
  public static void main(String args[]) {
    Date objDate = new Date( ); // Current System Date and time is assigned to objDate
    System.out.println(objDate);
    String strDateFormat = "hh:mm:ss a dd-MMM-yyyy";//Date format is Specified
    SimpleDateFormat objSDF = new SimpleDateFormat (strDateFormat);//Date format string is passed as an argument to the
Date format object
    System.out.println(objSDF.format(objDate));//Date formatting is applied to the current date
  }
}
```

Comparison of Dates

The most useful method of comparing dates is by using the method – compareTo()

Let us take a look at the below code snippet-

```
import java.text.SimpleDateFormat;
import java.text.ParseException;
import java.util.Date;

class TestDates_Compare{
public static void main(String args[]) throws ParseException{

SimpleDateFormat objSDF = new SimpleDateFormat("dd-mm-yyyy");
```

```
Date dt_1 = objSDF.parse("20-08-1981");
Date dt_2 = objSDF.parse("12-10-2012");

System.out.println("Date1 : " + objSDF.format(dt_1));
System.out.println("Date2 : " + objSDF.format(dt_2));

if (dt_1.compareTo(dt_2)>0){
System.out.println("Date 1 occurs after Date 2");
}// compareTo method returns the value greater than 0 if this Date is after the Date argument.

else if (dt_1.compareTo(dt_2)<0){
System.out.println("Date 1 occurs before Date 2");
}// compareTo method returns the value less than 0 if this Date is before the Date argument;

else if (dt_1.compareTo(dt_2)==0){
System.out.println("Both are same dates");
}// compareTo method returns the value 0 if the argument Date is equal to the second Date;
else{
System.out.println("You seem to be a time traveller !!");
}
}
}
```

How to use Java Timer and Example

Ways of Timer Java implementation
> 1) To set up a specific amount of delay until a task is executed.
> 2) To find the time difference between two specific events

Java Timer - Need to undersatnd Few concept

- It can only be a future event that can be timed.

- Will the event occur once or repeatedly?

- How long is the Timer required?

- There may be several Timers required in parallel.

- The timers should have the facility to stop or even cancel at any given point.

Java Timer Example

Using the Java timer for your programs

THE TIMER IN JAVA IS PROVIDED WITHIN THE <u>JAVA.UTIL</u> PACKAGE.

Let us have a look at using Timer for 2 tasks that we need to schedule-

Step 1) But before that lets create the class that will contain some task that we need to do-

```java
importjava.util.TimerTask;

importjava.util.Timer;

public class TaskMaster extends TimerTask{

    String strObject;

    publicTaskMaster(String strObject){

       this.strObject = strObject;

    }

    public void run(){

       System.out.println("Inside Run task-" + strObject);

    }
}
```

This is a simple class that uses the run() method of Threads when the task is invoked. The String strObject will help us identify which task is running.

Step 2) Create 2 timers as follows in a class called Java Timer class:

```java
Timer timer_1;

Timer timer_2;
```

Step 3) Create a constructor of this class having 2 integer parameters as input-

```java
public Timers(int t1,int t2) {
}
```

This constructor will have the code to invoke the 2 timers declared earlier to use for the tasks we created in TaskMaster class.

Step 4) Initiate the timers as follows –

timer_1 = new Timer();

Similarly do this for timer_2.

Step 5) Now if you use this timer object, you will see several methods in it.

We will first make use of the schedule method that takes in arguments as –

task - task to be scheduled.

delay - delay in milliseconds before task is to be executed.

period - time in milliseconds between successive task executions.

The delay and period will be the 2 integer arguments that we have passed in the constructor (created in step 3).

So the constructor now has the code as

timer_1 = new Timer();

timer_1.schedule(new TaskMaster("Alpha"), t1 * 1000, t1 * 1000);

Step 6) Repeat step 5 for timer_2 and pass some different string say "Delta".

Your constructor should now be looking something like-

```
public Timers(int t1,int t2) {

    timer_1 = new Timer();

    timer_1.schedule(new TaskMaster("Alpha"), t1 * 1000, t1 * 1000);

    //timer_1.scheduleAtFixedRate(new TaskMaster("Alpha"), t1 * 1000, t1 * 1000);

    timer_2 = new Timer();

    timer_2.schedule(new TaskMaster("Delta"), t2 * 1000, t2 * 1000);

    //timer_2.scheduleAtFixedRate(new TaskMaster("Delta"), t2 * 1000, t2 * 1000);

}
```

Ignore the commented lines for now. We shall see that after executing this code in step 8.

Step 7) Now create the main method and call the Timersclass with 2 arguments as integers.

```
public static void main(String args[]) {

new Timers(1,5);

}
```
Step 8) On executing this main method, the result will appear something like this-

Inside Run task-Alpha

Inside Run task-Alpha

Inside Run task-Alpha

Inside Run task-Alpha

Inside Run task-Delta

Inside Run task-Alpha

Inside Run task-Alpha

Inside Run task-Alpha

Inside Run task-Alpha

Inside Run task-Alpha

Inside Run task-Alpha

Inside Run task-Delta

Inside Run task-Alpha

Inside Run task-Alpha

Inside Run task-Alpha

...... THIS WILL CONTINUE UNTIL YOU DON'T TERMINATE THE PROGRAM.

This was the Schedule method of timer that schedules the specified task for repeated FIXED-DELAY EXECUTION, beginning after the specified delay. Subsequent executions take place at approximately regular intervals separated by the specified period.

In fixed-delay execution, each execution is scheduled RELATIVE TO THE ACTUAL EXECUTION TIME OF THE PREVIOUS EXECUTION

Step 9) Now comment the line with schedule method and uncomment the scheduleAtFixedRate.

The output will be quite similar.

This method too schedules the specified task for repeated FIXED-RATE EXECUTION, beginning after the specified delay. Subsequent executions take place at approximately regular intervals, separated by the specified period.

In fixed-rate execution, each execution is scheduled RELATIVE TO THE SCHEDULED EXECUTION TIME OF THE INITIAL EXECUTION.

Oh yes!! You can programmatically stop the timers by calling the cancel() method of the timer.

Made in the USA
Las Vegas, NV
16 March 2021